Language and the Law in Deaf Communities

Ceil Lucas, General Editor

Language and the Law

in Deaf

Communities

Ceil Lucas, Editor

GALLAUDET UNIVERSITY PRESS

Washington, D.C.

Sociolinguistics in Deaf Communities

A Series Edited by Ceil Lucas

Gallaudet University Press
Washington, D.C. 20002

http://gupress.gallaudet.edu

ISBN 1-56368-143-9
ISSN 1080-5494

Contents

Editorial Advisory Board

Introduction

Volume 9 of the Sociolinguistics in Deaf Communities series focuses on the area of forensic linguistics, that is, the area where language and the law intersect. As Roger Shuy (2001) points out, the use of the term *forensic linguistics* began in the 1980s and is now the accepted name for this area of study. Forensic linguistics has its own academic organization, The International Association of Forensic Linguistics, and its own journal, *Forensic Linguistics*. The focus of this volume is on where language and the law intersect in deaf communities, and as we see from each paper, this intersection is wide, deep, and of real consequence in the lives of everyday deaf people. Following Shuy's introduction to the issue of the language problems experienced by minorities in legal settings, the papers explore the interrogation of deaf people (Hoopes), interpretation issues for juries that include deaf people (Mather and Mather), and the basic issue of word meanings in lay and legal contexts (Geer). The volume concludes with a piece by a public defender with extensive experience in practicing and teaching law but no specialized training or knowledge of the legal problems of deaf people (Castelle), the point being to capture an informed outside perspective. It is the hope of the editor and the contributors that this book will be of interest and use not only to linguists but also to anyone involved with and interested in legal issues as they impact deaf people.

Since some of the authors in this book have not published in the area of sign sociolinguistics before, we are initiating a new tradition with the inclusion of brief author biographies. We will continue this tradition in subsequent volumes of the series.

I am grateful to the contributors, the members of the editorial board, and to Robert Bayley, David Penna and Risa Shaw for their work in putting this volume together. I also gratefully acknowledge Ivey Pittle Wallace, the assistant editorial director, Deirdre Mullervy, managing editor, and Doug Roemer, copy editor, at Gallaudet University Press for their support, hard work, and enduring sense of humor.

Ceil Lucas

The Language Problems of Minorities

in the Legal Setting

Roger W. Shuy

Virtually all people who have had the unfortunate experience of being accused of a crime are at an immediate disadvantage, especially if they are not guilty of some or all of the charges. They enter a new world of discourse, one that is strange and different from any other interaction they have ever encountered (Mellinkoff 1963; Tiersma 1999). Likewise, a person who brings a civil complaint faces a new and different world of language and culture. Their most important resource in such situations is a good attorney to guide them through the morass of legal experience. Their greatest problem is the distance they have from the specialized discourse of law enforcement and the courtroom. Those who can afford to, hire top notch lawyers. But even then, those whose language and culture are more distant from the language and culture of law usually have a serious problem, even on the rare occasions when they obtain excellent legal representation. Less affluent minorities simply suffer.

Decades of research on the rich variations found in American English dialects, and the everyday practical applications of such research have been limited largely to the classroom. By comparison, relatively little has been written about the problems Deaf people experience during the everyday tasks of their lives, including getting adequate medical treatment, negotiating the world of buying and selling, and, in this case, presenting and preserving themselves in the legal setting.

Differences in language go hand in hand with differences in culture, since language is an integral part of culture. The culture of the legal process is foreign to most Americans. Nowhere else do we need someone else to do our talking for us. Nowhere else are we prevented from introducing our own topics and telling our stories in our own way. Nowhere else are we forbidden to interrupt the other speaker or ask our own questions. Nowhere else must we be ever vigilant to the language traps posed by the other side. In short, nowhere else are we prevented from using our own ideas in our own voice. And if this is problematic for the average person, it is much more so for the inarticulate and less educated, the speaker of a different dialect, the speaker of a different language, and those who do not speak and hear at all.

The specialized discourse of the legal setting is the subject of this paper. The focus here is on the problems of language and cultural differences that minorities experience when they are interrogated in court and when they try to get their own interests represented at trial. Three types of minorities are discussed: people who speak a different social dialect, people who speak a language other than English, and people who may not speak at all: Deaf people. All three groups come to the legal context with similar problems. It is not my purpose to rank the differences in order of magnitude that these three groups have. Suffice it to say, these minorities share a great disadvantage, one that it is even greater than those faced by the average person. Over the past thirty years, I have helped attorneys represent hundreds of people, including some from each of these three categories.

THE LEGAL PROBLEMS OF A SPEAKER
OF HAWAIIAN CREOLE

When dialect speakers are required to make a court appearance, their speech often puts them at a disadvantage. The case of a young Creole speaker from Molokai Island, Hawaii, is a case in point. Steven Suyat was born into an impoverished family on a pineapple plantation. He had minimal education and spoke the local dialect. Eventually he became a carpenter and worked his way up in the local carpenter's union to become a union business agent. During a union action against a local non-union builder, the carpenter's union was accused of illegal picketing. Charges were brought against the president of that union, and Suyat, among others, was brought before a grand jury to be a hostile witness against his own boss. This put Suyat in a difficult position, especially since the police had not been able to find anything with which to charge him. Readers should be reminded that when people appear before a grand jury, they can have no attorney with them in the courtroom to help them navigate the complex proceedings.

The Multiple Meanings of Words

During his grand jury testimony, Suyat was asked questions that he believed he was answering truthfully, but these answers were taken by the prosecutor to be untruthful. Although Suyat had not been indicted up to that point, charges of perjury were subsequently brought against him (Shuy 1993).

His indictment contained six counts of perjury. One might think that this means that he was accused of six different lies. But one of the oddities of law, from a lay perspective at least, is that repetitions of the same alleged lie can be used as separate counts of perjury. Thus, the first four of the six counts against Suyat were all on the same point, the same bit of information. By asking the same question four times, the prosecutor increased the charges against him. The transcript of Suyat's trial testimony displays these four questions and his answers as follows:

Q: And one of the jobs of the business agent is to organize non-union contractors, isn't that right?
A: No.
Q: So no part of your job is to organize contractors?
A: No.
Q: And so no part of Mr. Nishibayashi's job is to organize contractors either?
A: That's right.
Q: And no part of Torres' job is to organize contractors?
A: That's right.

Although the union's attorney was waiting outside the grand jury courtroom and was available if Suyat should want to ask for a short recess to seek his advice, Suyat felt no need to ask his lawyer what a contractor was. He knew very well that a contractor is a builder who makes contracts with customers to erect houses. He also knew very well that people who work for contractors are carpenters.

He didn't know that the word, in this context at least, had more than one meaning. To Suyat, the union's job was to organize carpenters, not contractors, so he said "no" to all four of the prosecutor's questions. In his understanding of the word *contractor*, Suyat was telling the truth as far as he could tell. His legal difficulty came from the fact that the district attorney used the word *contractor* to refer to a contracting company, including its workers. The legal dialect of the prosecutor did not match Suyat's nonlegal understandings, but this did not make any difference. As far as the prosecutor was concerned, he had lied four times.

The fifth and sixth counts of his indictment were equally problematic. They too were repetitions, and his answer was judged to be the same alleged lie. In his grand jury testimony, he faced still another linguistic dilemma as well. The grand jury colloquy was as follows:

Q: What does the word *scab* mean?
A: I have no recollection.
Q: You don't know what the word *scab* means?
A: No.

Suyat had apparently written the word *scab* in the log book that he kept at his job as a business agent. As a business agent, he could be expected to know what it meant. But what did Suyat think he was being asked? The prosecutor's two questions on this topic are instructive. Suyat's answer, "I have no recollection," seems odd. Did he once know the meaning but then claim to have forgotten it? Was he claiming to never have known the meaning of a word that he wrote in his log? Or was something else in Suyat's mind here? The prosecutor fully understood that not being able to recall something does not constitute a charge for an indictment. So he pursued it further, asking if Suyat knew what it meant "now" (using the present tense), to which Suyat said, "No."

At least part of his problem was that Suyat seemed to think the questions meant something else. He later reported that he thought he was being asked to define the word, much in the way that a dictionary might define it. He knew that he was out of his league as a lexicographer. His meager schooling taught him never to try to answer a question he didn't know how to answer. A minute after this exchange, the prosecutor attempted to get clarification and asked, "You don't remember what you meant when you wrote it down here?" To this, Suyat replied, "Well, yeah," a reasonably clear indication that he did indeed remember what he meant by the word *scab* when he wrote it in his log book.

This clarification, or change in perspective about what the district attorney wanted, was used as evidence that Suyat had lied when he said earlier that he didn't know what *scab* meant. This yielded counts five and six of his indictment for perjury. Equally interesting is the fact that the prosecutor did not then ask Suyat, "Well, what *did* you mean by it?" This omission reveals his strategy of not really caring what Suyat said during his testimony as long as he could be caught in some kind of perjurious statement. It is sometimes the case that one purpose of grand jury testimony is to catch witnesses in a lie so that they can then be indicted.

The Culture of the Courtroom

Not only was Suyat disadvantaged by his different native Creole dialect and his relative lack of education but also by his total unfamiliarity with the culture of the courtroom and the different levels of meaning that the district attorney used on him. He was ultimately convicted of perjury on all six counts and served a year in prison (Shuy 1993).

THE LEGAL PROBLEMS OF A SPANISH SPEAKER

The case of Steven Suyat focused on problems of the minority speaker in the courtroom. Next, we examine the legal system's management of evidence used by a Spanish speaker in the process of bringing an indictment (Shuy 1992).

In March of 1986, the U.S. Customs Office seized 750 kilos of cocaine at a New Jersey port. The owners of the drugs were nowhere to be found, so Customs and the U.S. Drug Enforcement Agency decided to make a controlled delivery of a shipment of those drugs to a man that they suspected to be the intended recipient/owner. The government believed that if the person receiving that drug shipment simply accepted it, he would identify himself as part of the drug deal.

Therefore, about a week later, a truck drove up to a junkyard owned by the suspect. An undercover agent, posing as the driver, explained that drugs were hidden in a secret compartment of the trailer. The junkyard owner was an immigrant Spanish speaker from Mexico with very limited English. Immediately, he was brought in for questioning. He claimed to have no knowledge of the drugs and implicated a friend, another junk dealer, and he agreed to wear a hidden microphone and covertly record his conversations with the man he accused, his alleged friend. Two recordings were made, both in the native Mexican Spanish of both speakers. As a result, the second man was arrested.

Translation without Transcription

The usual procedure in criminal prosecutions is for the government to provide both the tapes and the transcripts of such evidence to the defense before trial. Not always, however, are such transcripts made in an appropriate manner (Berk-Seligson 1990; Wu 1995). In this case, the prosecutor provided two tapes in Spanish and two transcripts that were English translations. When the attorney called me to help on this case, my first question to him was, "Where are the Spanish transcripts of these tape recordings?" There were none, for the district attorney had simply hired someone to make a translation, and he relied on this English translation to make his case. The problem with this procedure, as any linguist knows, is that there is no way of knowing whether or not the translations are accurate.

Every law case in which different languages are tape-recorded and used as evidence should follow a three-step process in producing an English transcript to be used at trial (Shuy 1992; Wu 1995):

1. Prepare a transcript in the original language spoken.
2. Translate that language into English.
3. Provide both the Spanish transcript and the English translation to the defendant.

The defense should be given the product of all three steps. In this case, the prosecution provided only step two to the defense attorney.

To remedy this situation, the defense did what the prosecution should have done in the first place. It hired its own bilingual translator, who first produced a Spanish transcript and then an English translation of it. As one might suspect, the resultant English translation made by the defense contained many important differences from that of the prosecution. Once these differences were called to the judge's attention, he ordered both sides to provide both a Spanish transcript and an English translation of the tapes.

It is not uncommon in criminal cases in which tape recordings are used as evidence for transcript differences to be debated in a special hearing for that purpose. Sometimes judges, despite their lack of expertise in the languages used, translation principles, and linguistics, decide that one or the other of the transcripts is best. Sometimes they throw up their hands and let both sides present their own transcripts to the jury. This judge knew no Spanish himself, so he could think of no better solution than to force the prosecution and defense translators to meet and hash out their differences before trial. Not surprisingly, this was not very successful. No agreement could be reached by the two translators, resulting again in two different sets of documents. Finally, the judge permitted each side to use its own version of the English transcript at trial.

But things got even worse. The cooperating witness, the man who wore the microphone, was also currently under investigation for the theft of a tractor trailer containing brass rods stolen from Connecticut. A few years earlier, he had been convicted of aggravated assault, resisting arrest, and illegal possession of firearms. He was already in deep trouble when the police convinced him to tape-record his friend. By wearing the microphone, he had hopes of reducing his recent theft charges. Under such circumstances, it always behooves the cooperating witness to help the government by succeeding in netting another suspect during his covert tape-recording task. If he were to fail, he'd lose the benefit of his cooperation and face even more jail time.

So, if the man he is taping does not come out with statements that self-generate his own guilt, the cooperating witness can try two other strategies. One is to be vague and ambiguous in such a way the police will infer that his friend is actually guilty. The other is to retell the events and try to get his friend to agree or at least not to disagree. The cooperating witness tried both strategies, never with total success. Nevertheless, he testified against his friend before a grand jury, claiming that he himself was an innocent bystander and his friend was the intended recipient of the drug shipment.

Before the criminal trial started, the cooperating witness dropped dead of a heart attack. This was bad news for the defense, since there would now be no opportunity to cross-examine him. The defense attorney now had to deal with the dead man's accusation before the grand jury, two hard-to-hear tapes, a defective government translation, and no cooperating witness to question and impeach.

During the trial that followed, the defense was allowed to use its own translation to counter the many errors in the prosecution's version. Additional linguistic analysis included topic and response analyses, commonly carried out in cases in which conversation is the evidence (Shuy 1982, 1990, 1993). Comparison of the salient topics raised by the cooperating witness and the defendant showed no self-generated guilt on the defendant's part. In fact, the defendant's question "What is your cut?"

indicated that he not only didn't understand the "cut" reference but also that the cut in question was the cooperating witness's, not the defendant's (see figure 1).

The questions that a person asks also provide a clue to what they know or do not know. The cooperating witness asked eight questions about the truck and the papers, indicating that even he lacked insider knowledge of the events that transpired.

Mistranslation

Once the court required the government to provide a Spanish transcript, it was discovered that it contained considerably more Spanish words than did the defense transcript. When the two different Spanish transcripts were finally compared, it was discovered that the government's translator was Cuban, whereas the speakers on the tape were Mexican. Some of the words that the government's translator thought he heard and then transcribed were Spanish terms that were unique to Cuban Spanish but were not used by Mexicans. In light of these obvious mistakes, the defense attorney requested and ultimately got an audibility hearing to bring this issue to light. As a result, much of the government's transcript was discredited and redacted.

It should also be noted that when the government produces tape recordings as evidence in trials, the law requires that someone authenticate the tapes. If the person wearing the microphone is a law enforcement

Topics Introduced

By cooperating witness	By defendant, his friend
Those people are pestering me, trying to pick it up. (8)	Let him go pick it up. (6)
They say they showed me the truck and the pictures. (5)	What is your cut? (1)
It came to me. (2)	What's in the newspaper? (4)
They took possession. (2)	It can't be done. (3)
They didn't give me anything. (1)	
I don't have the papers. (1)	

FIGURE 1. *Comparison of topics, including the number of times these topics were raised by the cooperating witness and the defendant*

officer, he or she is normally the one who appears in court to identify the speakers' voices (speaker identification is not always easy in such cases), the dates, the times, and the locations of the tapings, and the recording equipment used. When the person wearing the microphone is a cooperating witness, as in this case, he or she is normally called upon for the same task. But when no government agent is present at the taping event and the cooperating witness dies before trial, the only possible authenticators are the agents who were monitoring those conversations at some distant point and who moved in to make the arrest at the very end of the conversations. Suffice it to say, they were neither fluent Spanish speakers nor linguists.

Even if these monitoring agents could hear and understand the conversations, they would have difficulty identifying who was speaking at a given time and what was said, especially since their knowledge of Mexican Spanish was deficient. In this case, the only remaining authenticator was the government's translator. But, as has been explained above, the translator's procedure was badly flawed.

Only upon the court's insistence did he produce a Spanish transcript, and even then it was discovered that he apparently guessed at many expressions that were not audible on the tape. In short, he fell far short of following the proper practice of a translator, and he went far beyond the limits provided by the actual taped data. Because of these shortcomings, the judge agreed with most of the defense attorney's objections, and redacted many of the imperfectly transcribed and then imperfectly translated passages.

Ambiguity

The curious thing about the entire indictment was that it was based on the government's interpretation of ambiguous and vague expressions used by both men. Crucial passages that were given a sinister interpretation by the prosecutor include the following exchanges between the cooperating witness (CW) and the friend (F):

CW: *That shithead* has been calling me trying to collect from me for *that thing.* Well, I didn't owe anything. *They* sent it to me but I don't . . .

F: *Have* him go pick it up, because *the paper* is there, you and he.

*   *   *

CW: *These people* are harassing me and then kicking me in the ass. I'm the one with *the main one.* And I'm nobody.

*   *   *

CW: *They* have *it* there. The same day *it* arrived, the following day *they took it away.*

*   *   *

F: Tell *him* to go to the Feds and pick *it* up. Tell *him* where *it* is and everything. "Look, hey, you go to such and such a place, go there, they are going to turn *it* over to you. Go claim *it* there if *it's* yours."

CW: No but *it* came directly to me, to my company.

F: Well, yes, that's fine, but the Feds take it there. "I don't have to pick that up." If there's *something* outstanding, send the bill to the Feds. You understand? And let *him* go and claim the container. Who owns that? Where is *that company?* I sure would have gone over and said, "I received *it* here, but just as I received *it* here, *it* was taken away by the Feds." You understand? The hell with it. Complain *there.*

There is reason to believe that the *it* frequently mentioned by the men refers to a compartment in which the drugs were hidden. But *it* could also refer to the whole trailer in which the drugs came. It would have been nice to be able to straighten this out.

If anything, the CW's reference to the *shithead* who keeps calling him to collect *that thing* suggests that he, the CW, knows who this is and that he may have been the intended recipient of the shipment. The friend's responses indicate that he is not personally involved. He offers advice, not directives: "Have him go pick it up," "Tell him . . . " and "I sure would have gone over and said . . . "

Even more interesting is the fact that the CW's own words seem to indicate that he, not the friend, is the one involved: "I'm the one with the main one" and "It came directly to me, to my company." The CW does not say, "We're the main ones" and "It came directly to us." Nor does he say, "You're the main one" and "It came directly to you."

Likewise, the friend's language makes it clear that he is not the one involved in this: "you and he" and "Tell him . . . " The friend does not say, "us and he" and "We should tell him . . . " The friend's stance is as a third-party observer, asking questions and giving advice to another person, rather than as a participant.

Notice also that there are quotation marks in these passages, indicating constructed dialogue used by the friend. The government's transcript treated these passages as though they were the words of the friend, not his constructed dialogue of what the friend tells the CW to say to the *shithead*.

Neither the Spanish nor the English translations clarify enough of these conversations to enable us to determine who the people are that are pestering the cooperating witness, exactly what they were speaking about, or what and who is referenced by his use of *it* and *they*. And since the cooperating witness had died, there was no way to ask him. These uses of *him* and *it* were discussed at trial, but unfortunately for the defendant, he was still left with the government's contention that he was personally involved in the deal.

It is not unusual for the prosecution to infer its own interpretation of the meaning of ambiguities; however, when the defendant is a speaker of another language, the prosecutor has an even greater burden. It was problematic for the defense attorney to put his client on the stand in his own defense, even through an interpreter, for the possibilities of his being confused and trapped by the subtleties of cross-examination language were very great. In this case, the defense attorney had to bet on the jury's ability to evaluate the prosecution's interpretation of the ambiguities in favor of the defense. Had the cooperating witness lived, the attorney might have been able to impeach his testimony. Had the judge allowed a linguistic expert witness to take the stand, the significance and impact of such ambiguities might have been revealed. But the judge did not allow me to testify and the client was convicted of involvement in a narcotics transaction.

THE LEGAL PROBLEMS OF A DEAF MAN

Most of us are uncomfortable when we try to buy an automobile, for this is an event in which most buyers are disadvantaged by the process, the conventions, and the technicalities of the task. Multiply this disadvantage by ten for a Deaf customer.

In 1987, a young man named Mitchell Bien walked into a large new car dealership in Fort Worth to find out the price of a new model car.

Bien had been raised by a hearing family, who had managed his interactions with the hearing world since birth. His father had recently died, however, and the family pick-up truck was not to Mitchell's mother's liking. She sent her son out to scout for a new car with which she would be more comfortable. The logical first step was to get a general idea of what this would cost.

When Bien entered the dealership, the salesperson recognized that he was Deaf and they began to write notes back and forth. By the time they had finished, they had produced 101 four-by-four sheets of exchanges. After being kept there for over four hours and being treated badly, Bien was very angry, and he went into the salesperson's office and snatched up the note sheets.

The next day, Bien sought out an attorney to bring charges against the dealership. The charges were negligence, gross negligence, false imprisonment, infliction of emotional distress, fraud, violations of the Texas Deceptive Trade Practices Act, and violations against the Texas Human Resources code for the protection of handicapped people.

So what was the evidence for these charges? The note sheets offered convincing proof. The exchanges show that after Bien wrote that he was there to price a new car only, the salesperson ignored this completely and convinced Bien to give up his truck keys so that their assessor could determine its trade-in value. Next, he produced a document called a "computer price and equipment confirmation form" and began to fill in various lines, including "buyer's allowance," "cash down," "remainder due," and "monthly payments." Nowhere on this form was any indication that this was a contract of any type. The salesperson told Bien that he would need to take it to the sales manager for approval and/or negotiations. The salesperson added, however, that the manager would surely make a better deal for Bien if he would give him a check for $4,000 to carry to the manager's office as evidence of the seriousness of his interest. Bien dutifully complied by providing both his truck keys and a check, and this is where the bad treatment began.

The dealership's defense was that they had no idea that Bien only wanted to price a new vehicle. They further asserted that they had made an offer and that he had made a counteroffer, all normal in an everyday car transaction. They also denied that Bien had indicated that he wanted to leave, that they prevented his leaving, and that they had done anything to upset him. In preliminary hearings, the dealership claimed that if the note sheets were placed in "proper sequence," they would show "a quite different picture" than Bien presented. The only documentation for what transpired and how long Bien was at the dealership came from the notes themselves.

Using a Linguist to Represent a Client

It was clear to the attorney that a trial would turn on the two different interpretations of what happened during the event at the dealership, what the note sheets meant, and how the note sheets were sequenced. As in the case of the Spanish speaker described above, putting Bien on the stand would create a series of potential problems. Like most people, he was unfamiliar with the culture of the courtroom, and he was seriously handicapped by not being able to hear or speak English. That meant that he would need to have an American Sign Language (ASL) interpreter, but Bien's ASL was less than adequate because he had been raised and protected by hearing parents in an all-hearing world. Bien's attorney needed a spokesperson for his client, someone who could speak on his behalf. He had heard about linguistics and its past uses at trial, so he called me.

Bien's attorney asked me if I could analyze the note sheets and put them in a reasonably certain chronological order, or "proper sequence." I agreed to do this by carrying out a speech event analysis to provide the basic time units in which the note sheets could be placed. Although there are many human activities in which speech occurs, only a small number of them are definable as speech events; that is, those events in which the speech used defines and constitutes that event. People may converse while walking through a park, but the event of walking though a park is not sufficiently specific or definable for us to prescribe the speech as "a walking through the park speech event." In contrast, well-defined events such as an interview, courtroom testimony, a medical history, a lecture, or a sales encounter contain specific and predictable speech routines that define such events for what they are.

On the basis of my earlier research on the structure of a business proposal event (Shuy 1987), I constructed the basic phases of a car sales event as follows:

1. Introduction/greeting phase
2. Customer's needs and preferences ascertained by salesperson phase

      a.   Determine customer's financial profile

      b.   Avoid mentioning price

3. Display product phase

      a.   Showroom displays

      b.   Test drive

      c.   Hospitality (coffee, etc.)

4. Make offer phase

      a.   Discuss trade-in value

      b.   Dealer makes first offer

      c.   Customer makes counteroffer

      d.   Salesperson joins with customer against "bad guy" manager

5. Completion of sale phase

      a.   Verbal agreement

      b.   Signed contract

      c.   Money down

6. Closing/leaving phase

Along with obvious time references, such as "you told me earlier," the content of the 101 non-numbered note slips guided the placement of each slip into the appropriate phase of a car sales event. Important to this case, such sequencing and numbering of the note slips enabled me to determine whether or not the claims of innocence by the defendant were accurate. Did the event ever reach the negotiation stage? Was Bien prevented from leaving when he wanted to, and if so, when? Were his rights violated?

Examination of the chronologically numbered note slips show that Bien complained many times and that at least four hours had elapsed:

42: I have been here for an hour so they cook dinner I got home and this got cold.

46: I have gone now because my brother looking at me too long.

56: I don't want to waiting so long here.

64: I have been here for two three hours so I'm tired now.

75: I'm already little crazy man because you both held me to stay.

77: You can't hold me to stay here too long for 4 hours because I already been here for 4 hours.

It is not uncommon for automobile salespersons to leave their customers alone in a cubicle for long periods of time while alleged negotiations take place with their sales managers for a better deal. It is hopefully uncommon for this to happen over a four-hour period with a reluctant customer. It is hopefully even more uncommon for the customer to have to ask over and over again to get his check back, all the time having his request refused:

40: If I write my check then you will return it back.
46: Please return my check now.
47: Please return my check now!
56: Where is my check?
60: Where is my check?
61: Please listen me, please return my check.
62: You say you will bring it back after your boss see it but you won't bring it back.
64: Tell your boss please return my check.
65: Please bring it back.
71: Show me where is your boss's office.
72: If you won't show his office go straight to police dept.
77: Please give me my check Right Now.
79: Please gave me my check back NOW.

Bien also complained about not feeling well.

49: My brain still confuse so let me get home for need some rest.
52: I'm not good feel now.
61: I'm little pressure myself. Please let me go home for rest.
63: I'm not ready to buy because they make me feel a little crazy.
64: I'm tired now.
65: I'm not very well.
71: I'm already a little crazy man.

Did Bien ever make a counteroffer, a sure indication that would indicate that he actually came in to purchase a new car and that there were serious negotiations going on? Bien's own words during the meeting indicated otherwise. The closest he comes to this is to offer the contingency that if they should make him a good deal, he will think about it.

39: If good deal and I will call my Insurance then come back here.
40: If good deal then go to home and call my Insurance for how much cost for that car.
41: Rather my brother (In response to salesperson's offer to let Bien call his insurance agent from the dealership).

42: I can't buy it right now.
46: I will come over here if you mail me a letter of good deal.
47: You can't push me to buy.

Did this sales event reach the point at which negotiations about price or counteroffers took place? Again, we have Bien's own words to tell us otherwise.

42: I can't buy it right now.
43: Not worth.
44: If I buy now I still lose $2,775.00 for my truck.
45: He gave me too high price and lose my money for truck is price.
47: You can't push me to buy.
48: I don't like his idea price.
50: I don't like your boss for deal.
51: I have gone now
52: Forget it.
53: Forget that.
63: I'm not ready to buy.
65: I will not buy today.
74: I don't accept your deal!

The note sheets make it very clear that Bien never accepted the dealer's offer, never made a counteroffer, repeatedly asked for his check back, and told both the salesperson and the sales manager that he didn't feel well and wanted to go home. At one point, Bien reports that he asked for his truck keys back and the smiling salesman blocked the exit, dangling the car keys in front on him.

In the end, Bien was more fortunate than many minorities who try to survive legal battles. He had a good attorney, help from a linguist, a poor defense of an untenable position by the dealership, and a sympathetic jury who ruled in his favor and awarded him $6 million dollars in damages.

CONCLUSION

These three case studies are illustrative of the problems minorities face in an American legal setting unforgiving of cultural and language differences. Even the average citizen lives in a world very different from the culture of the courtroom. But minority citizens are even farther away from such a culture, so far, in fact, that their chance of being successful in expressing and defending themselves is depressingly low.

Even the experienced expert witness must be on guard at all times for the types of questions that the Hawaiian Creole speaker, Steven Suyat, faced in his grand jury testimony. One has to anticipate the significance of the expressions used by attorneys and the ever-present danger of answering multipart questions (which should be objected to but not always are). In short, one has to learn to believe that the opposing attorney is not your friend. Sadly, one also has to learn that the point of the trial is seldom to achieve justice, but rather to win at any cost.

The case of the New Jersey Mexican American man who spoke little or no English shows how important it is to be able to point out the difference between explicitness and ambiguity and the obvious need to have a foreign language transcript, not just an English translation of it. Perhaps more important, this case clearly points to the need for a linguist to assist the triers of the fact. Such assistance was denied by the judge, and the defendant is now spending the rest of his life in prison.

The case of the Deaf man, Mitchell Bien, is a more hopeful one. The judge permitted the linguist to represent the interests of a man who would undoubtedly have been destroyed by cross-examination by the opposing attorney. Credit should also be given to Bien's attorney, who had the foresight to call on a linguist for help.

Something also should be said about the role of a linguist in such cases. Linguistic analysis is not advocacy. That is the role of the attorney. Linguists analyze the language data and reach conclusions about it that would be the same no matter which side uses it. Trial testimony is simply reporting the results of such analysis. Linguists stay away from the ultimate issues of who is right and who is wrong, no matter how tempting it is to feel outraged by the other side's position.

In Suyat's case, the linguist's job would have been to point out the multiple understandings that the prosecutor's ambiguous words could have produced. This is not to say that linguistics can, in any way, determine what Suyat actually understood. Nobody but Suyat could know this. But the structure of language reveals multiple meanings that are possible. That's as far as the linguist can go. If communication involves a sender, a message, and a receiver, the linguist deals only with the *possible* intention and understanding inherent in the structure of the message.

In the Mexican American man's case, the linguist's job would have been much the same—pointing out how the ambiguous nouns and pronouns in those texts have nonexplicit references and are subject to different interpretations by later listeners. Again, the focus of linguistic testimony, had it been allowed, would have been on the message, not on what the sender actually meant or on what the receiver actually understood.

In Mitchell Bien's case, such testimony was permitted by the judge, who seems to have understood that the linguist would not go beyond the boundaries authorized by the legal setting.

These cases provide a sharp contrast in the experiences of minorities in the American courtroom. The message is: Although all legal laypersons face a very different culture when they go to court, the difficulty of minorities is far greater than for those who speak and hear the English language. One solution to this problem, which is currently in partial practice, is to have an interpreter present at trial. Even if the interpreter is competent, such a solution is partial at best. Minorities who are fortunate enough to have a linguist on their side, analyzing the language data and presenting their findings at trial, face a fairer outcome.

THE SPECIAL PROBLEMS OF DEAF PEOPLE

The papers in this book delve more deeply into the special problems faced by Deaf people with law enforcement and the courts in the contexts of police interrogations of Deaf suspects, courtroom interpretation for Deaf jurors, and the interpretations that have been imposed on key terms in the Americans with Disabilities Act.

Police Interrogations of Deaf Suspects

Hoopes shows how ASL is a fully developed language in its own right. Readers unfamiliar with the amazing complexity and beauty of ASL can only be convinced that Deaf people, who use it as their native language, are disadvantaged in legal settings, such as police interrogations, in which only the feeblest of efforts are made by law enforcement to ensure that Deaf suspects understand what they are being asked and that they understand their constitutional rights. Hoopes grounds his observations in research that offers clear evidence that beginning or even intermediate-level interpreters do this poorly. Only advanced-level interpreters are adequate for this task. Hoopes is quite vocal when he calls the current situation the "trampling of Deaf Americans' constitutional rights."

Interpretation for Deaf Jurors

Mather and Mather examine the use of interpreters for Deaf jurors during trials. The authors show how the courts hold gross misunderstandings about the important differences between ASL and Signed English. Citing actual court rulings, they point out how the courts assert that the only way for interpreters to accomplish the task of conveying the meaning of spoken English at trial is for such interpreters to use Signed English, not ASL, despite the fact that Deaf speakers' ability with English is notoriously weak.

We can only wonder why the courts are consistent in permitting monolingual Spanish-speaking jurors, for example, to benefit from Spanish interpreters while, at the same time, denying Deaf jurors the right to benefit from interpretations in their own native ASL. Perhaps part of the problem lies with the use of the word *interpreter*. When I testify for the defense in a criminal case, I am sometimes accused of merely "interpreting" language use when I carry out a linguistic analysis. This appears to be an obvious ploy to impeach my testimony by referring to it as a subjective interpretation rather than as an objective scientific analysis. In their paper, Mather and Mather argue for standards of "functional equivalency and meaning-based translation." One wonders if referring to what the interpreter does as a "translation" may set better in the legal context. After all, the courts already accept translations.

Problems with Key Terms in Federal Legislation for Deaf People

Geer's paper deals with specific key words and concepts found in federal legislation relating to Deaf Americans, particularly in the Americans with Disabilities Act of 1990, Section 504 of the Rehabilitation Act of 1973, and the Individuals with Disabilities in Education Act, pointing out that it is bad enough that the language of law is not clear to laypersons in general, but that it has dire consequences for Deaf people. The legal language omnipresent in the lives of everyone counts more heavily against Deaf people, who encounter it daily with credit card applications, medical consent forms, wills, the paperwork involved in purchasing and financing cars and homes, and even with parking violations.

Even to the hearing population, legal language is, as Peter Tiersma puts it, "decidedly peculiar and often hard to understand, especially from the perspective of the lay public" (Tiersma 1999, 2). How much more peculiar and hard to understand is this language to the Deaf population, who do not even share the base English concepts involved in terms such as *equal, reasonable,* and *rights.* Geer compares ASL understandings of these and other key terms with the expected understandings in the legal world. Is a person's "right" something that is mandatory? Or is it permissive? ASL offers different understandings than much of legal language anticipates. The same is true for "equality" and many other legal terms and concepts discussed by Geer.

This book introduces and promotes awareness of some of the difficult linguistic issues of the legal context facing Deaf Americans as they go about their task of everyday living.

REFERENCES

Berk-Seligson, S. 1990. *The bilingual courtroom.* Chicago: University of Chicago Press.

Mellinkoff, D. 1963. *The language of the law.* Boston: Little, Brown.

Shuy, R. W. 1982. Topic as the unit of analysis in a criminal law case. In *Analyzing discourse: Text and talk,* ed. D. Tannen, 113–26. Washington, D.C.: Georgetown University Press.

———. 1990. The analysis of tape recorded conversations. In *Criminal intelligence analysis,*ed. P. Andrews and M. Peterson, 117–48. Loomis, Calif.: Palmer Press.

———. 1992. Bilingual evidence in a U.S. criminal court case. *Plurilingua* 8: 165–73.

———. 1993. *Language crimes.* Cambridge: Blackwell.

———. 1994. Deceit, distress and false imprisonment: The anatomy of a car sales event. *Forensic Linguistics* 1(2):133–49.

———. 1995. Dialect as evidence in law cases. *Journal of English Linguistics* 23(1–2):195–208.

Tiersma, P. 1999. *Legal language.* Chicago: University of Chicago Press.

Wu, W. 1995. Chinese evidence versus the institutional power of English. *Forensic Linguistics* 2(2):154–65.

Trampling *Miranda:*

Interrogating Deaf Suspects

Rob Hoopes

Society knows very well how to oppress a man and has methods more subtle than death. (André Gide, *In Memoriam Oscar Wilde*)

The government's ability to arrest and interrogate an individual suspected of having committed a crime is a police power fundamental to maintaining the social harmony of a society. But, for the individual who suddenly finds himself forcibly restrained, isolated from the outside world, and subjected to questioning by the police, police interrogation can be terrifying, rendering the individual susceptible to misunderstandings, misstatements, and manipulation. When the individual arrested is Deaf, the linguistic and cultural gulf that separates him from his hearing accusers compounds his sense of fear and isolation. As a result, the Deaf suspect is all the more likely to misstate facts, to unwittingly agree to suggested statements and scenarios that imply culpability, and to make false confessions. Such statements, even if recanted, are often used at a later trial to persuade a jury that the individual committed a crime.

In 1966, the U.S. Supreme Court recognized that an arrested individual—afraid, alone, and under the compulsive pressure of police questioning—can easily be led into making false statements. The danger that such compulsion poses to the truth-seeking process and to our rights as individuals to be free from inordinate governmental pressure during the criminal process led the Court to a landmark decision. In *Miranda v. Arizona,* (384 U.S. 436, 86 S.Ct. 1602), the Supreme Court held that prior to interrogating an individual who has been taken into custody, the police must inform the individual of certain constitutional rights. This explanation, known as the *Miranda* warning, reminds the suspect that he has the right to remain silent (per the Fifth Amendment) and the right to the assistance of counsel (per the Sixth Amendment). The Court reasoned that knowledge of these rights, that is, knowing that one need not answer questions posed by the police and knowing that one may consult with an attorney at any time before or during interrogation, will reduce somewhat the sense of isolation, fear, and duress, which renders individuals susceptible to suggestion and manipulation.

The question this study addresses is whether Deaf Americans are afforded the same knowledge and understanding prior to and during police interrogation as hearing Americans. If a Deaf individual who uses American Sign Language (ASL) to communicate is not provided with a sign language interpreter at all during the reading of the *Miranda* rights or subsequent interrogation, he or she has obviously not been informed of his or her rights. Accordingly, any subsequent statements made by the Deaf suspect—whether written, gestured, signed, or vocalized—must be excluded from a later trial. A linguistic study is unnecessary to resolve this simple legal question.

The more difficult question is whether a Deaf person who has been provided an interpreter understands her rights and, therefore, can avail herself of their protections to the same extent as a hearing American. What effect does the level of interpreting competence have on the ability to interpret linguistically complex discourse such as the *Miranda* warning and police interrogation? Police, court administrators, and judges are largely uninformed that this is even an issue. The grave consequence of this understandable ignorance is that the *Mirandizing* and subsequent interrogation of Deaf suspects is routinely interpreted by individuals who lack the skill necessary to achieve either a clear understanding in Deaf defendants of their constitutional rights or the questions posed to them during interrogation.

This study examines the interpreted discourse of nine hearing individuals at various levels of interpreting skill—beginning, intermediate, and advanced. Their signed interpretations of the *Miranda* warning and an interrogation of a defendant by an attorney were analyzed and compared with regard to two linguistic features: (1) the number of correct lexical items produced and (2) the number of appropriate syntactic markers accomplished through nonmanual signals (i.e., through specific facial and head postures). The findings were dramatic. Skill level had a profound effect on the production of both of these linguistic features.

These findings were mirrored by a separate study of comprehensibility as determined by native Deaf signers. Ten Deaf individuals who acquired ASL as infants and who use it as their primary means of communication rated each of the signed interpretations for comprehensibility. The signed interpretations of the beginning signers were uniformly found to be incomprehensible. The signed interpretations of the intermediate signers were found to be incomprehensible at worst and confusing at best. The signed interpretations of the advanced interpreters were largely found to be fairly clear.

Finally, an ethnographic examination of a criminal case involving a Deaf suspect was conducted. This study included extensive interviews and language testing of the Deaf suspect while the case was still pending, an interview of the attorney representing the Deaf suspect, and a review of court documents relating to whether the alleged confession should be suppressed (i.e., excluded from evidence at a later trial). In short, this examination indicated that a police officer, who had taken less than ten weeks of ASL, had attempted to interpret the linguistically complex *Miranda* rights and the subsequent interrogation. The Deaf suspect did not understand the *Miranda* rights—either as it was signed or in the written English form—nor did he understand the subsequent interrogation. Nevertheless, the police in this case alleged that the defendant had understood and waived all of his constitutional rights and that he had confessed to the crime of rape. Later interviews with the attorneys, as well as certified interpreters, indicated that the practice of using policemen with limited signing skills to interpret the *Mirandizing* and subsequent interrogation of Deaf suspects is the modus operandi of the police in the Cincinnati metropolitan area.

Although this study deals with legal rights and processes, prior knowledge of law is not necessary to understand the information contained herein. Legal concepts and procedures are explained as plainly and as simply as possible. In addition, it is important that legal processes, such as police interrogation, not be viewed with too much reverence. The criminal justice system is an integral part of our culture and, as such, should reflect and give meaning to our cultural norms of fairness and equality.

THE LEGAL LANDSCAPE

Police Power and Human Rights: The Civilized Constraint of an Extraordinary Power

A civilizing bulwark of a civilized society is its criminal justice system. It is the societal institution that encourages adherence to a society's prescribed behaviors and avoidance of proscribed behaviors, a crucial endeavor for maintaining social harmony. Enforcing a society's norms is necessarily predicated on the ability to use brute force against individuals. Arrest, incarceration, taking of property, labeling someone a criminal—all are necessary for the task of maintaining social harmony. But, these police powers, if not constrained, can be intentionally or unintentionally misused against an individual, placing citizens in constant fear of being suddenly and arbitrarily persecuted. The philosopher John Locke explains that such misuse would amount to a taking of an individual's inalienable right to be free of arbitrary persecution by the government or by other men. It is the protection of these inalienable rights that forms the basis for our submission to government's power over us. When the state no longer is constrained in such a way to protect these natural rights, the social contract between the individual and his or her government has been violated (Sahakian 1968, 154–55).

The civilizing nature of a criminal justice system is determined by its procedures, that is, how a person suspected of a crime is processed through the truth-seeking process, starting with arrest and ending with the completion of punishment. When it appears a crime has been committed, the criminal process seeks to accomplish three fundamental goals. First, investigators search for relevant evidence to determine what occurred and who is responsible. Second, if from the evidence it appears, or in legal terms there is "probable cause to believe," a crime has been committed and that a particular individual committed it, there must be an analysis of the relevant information. In the United States, this is accomplished by trial, whereby a jury analyzes the relevant information (i.e., the evidence) presented to them, aided by the lawyers' elucidating (or obfuscating) reviews of the evidence (closing arguments). Third, if the trial indicates the defendant has committed a crime, punishment must be meted out. Punishment can take the form of a confiscation of property (a fine), liberty (imprisonment), or life (execution).

Clearly, the ability of the government to investigate crime, determine guilt, and punish offenders is crucial to maintaining social harmony. But it is also a power that permits the government to unleash its awesome resources, including the use of brute force, against a single individual.

The Power to Arrest and Interrogate

Imagine . . . you are stopping for gas on your way home from work. You're in a hurry. It has been a busy and tiring day. But the kids will be home from school and will be alone if you don't get there soon. You buy gas as quickly as you can. But, just as you are pulling away, a police car pulls in front of you, blocking your path. You sit, confused and staring at the flashing police lights. Two officers get out of the police cruiser and approach your car. As you are fumbling to roll down your window, you hear one of the approaching police officers say in a loud, stern voice, "Get out of the car!" "OK, but why?" you ask. "Get out of the car now!" is the response. You get out, and the officer tells you to put your hands on top of the car. Confused and stunned, you feel the officer's hands move down your body as he searches you. "You're under arrest," he says. Arrest? You feel the handcuffs on your wrists and hear the snap as they lock. You try to think about what is happening, but fear and shock have washed over you. You have a vague sense of people staring as you are placed in the back of the police cruiser. You stare out the window as the cruiser pulls out of the gas station where your car is still sitting at the pump. You think about your kids. And questions start running through your mind. Why is this happening? What will happen next? What should I do?

Several things happen at the moment a police officer takes a person into custody. The individual immediately, and without warning, loses important freedoms—to move about, to speak with others, to associate with others—depriving him of the social, emotional, and physical resources of his own individual world and of the larger world. Arrest also initiates an adversarial relationship between the individual and the government. Suddenly, the incredible resources of the government are directed against the individual for the purpose of obtaining a confession or conviction of the suspected crime. Arrest immediately places the individual's future liberty in jeopardy. The individual may realize that if innocence cannot be shown, he or she may be labeled a criminal, fined, incarcerated, and, in some circumstances, killed.

The focusing of governmental power, the acutely unequal social dynamic of an individual being isolated and confronted by police, and the risk of a criminal penalty can loom over an individual like a raised fist over a frightened child. These dynamics have made police interrogation such an effective tool in law enforcement, allowing police to ferret out information from individuals who would otherwise be unwilling to provide any. But its compulsive nature renders the individual vulnerable and easily led into agreeing to things which later, when viewed suspiciously through the lens of alleged criminality, may appear quite incriminating.

In sum, arrest and interrogation are invaluable and indispensable tools for law enforcement. But, by its very nature, interrogation is also subject to overreaching, and even abuse. Even absent overreaching, the coercive nature of interrogation while being held in police custody can lead innocent individuals into making untoward statements that later can appear to be incriminating.

Constraining the Power to Interrogate: The Fifth and Sixth Amendments

The Bill of Rights provides American citizens with a breathtaking spectrum of individual freedoms and protections from governmental interference. Two of these rights—the Fifth Amendment right against self-incrimination and the Sixth Amendment right to counsel in criminal proceedings—are particularly relevant to the interrogation of an individual in police custody.

The ultimate goal of the police in interrogating an individual is to obtain a complete confession to the alleged crime. If a complete confession cannot be obtained, the secondary goal is to obtain incriminating statements that may be used with other evidence to later convict him or her. The Fifth Amendment, however, guarantees that no person shall be compelled in a criminal case to be a witness against himself. Within the context of interrogation, this right means that the individual being interrogated need not speak or cooperate with the police. He or she has a right to remain silent.

Also highly relevant to custodial interrogation is the right to counsel. The Sixth Amendment provides that an individual accused of a crime has a right to counsel, that is, the right to consult with an attorney during all criminal proceedings. Since custodial interrogation of a suspected individual IS a criminal proceeding, an individual has the right to speak with an attorney before or at any time during police interrogation. As pointed out previously, arrest immediately isolates an individual from the outside world, cutting him off from informational, emotional, and physical resources. But the ability to speak with an attorney before or anytime during interrogation goes a long way to bringing the individual back from such isolation, and therefore, removes some of the coercive nature of the procedure. An individual has the right to the effective assistance of counsel even if she cannot afford the fees charged by private attorneys. In these cases, the government must appoint one for her free of charge (*Johnson v. Zerbst,* 304 U.S. 458, 58 S.Ct. 1019, 82 L.Ed. 1461 [1938]).

Clearly, the Fifth and Sixth Amendments provide protections that help to level the very un-level playing field of custodial interrogation. But, rights unknown are no better than no rights at all. For the protections contained within the Fifth and Sixth Amendments to be meaningful, the individual must be aware of what they are vis-à-vis police interrogation, when they may be exercised, and how they must be asserted. It was precisely this point which led the U.S. Supreme Court to its landmark 1966 decision: *Miranda v United States,* 384 U.S. 436, 86 S.Ct. 1602. The Court held that police must inform individuals of their Fifth and Sixth Amendment rights prior to interrogation. The litany that police officers recite is known as the *Miranda warning.* An individual who has been read these rights is sometimes described as having been *Mirandized.*

The *Miranda* warning (with slight modifications in certain jurisdictions) is as follows:

You have the right to remain silent.
Anything you say can and will be used against you in a court of law.
You have the right to talk to a lawyer and have him present with you while you are being questioned.
If you cannot afford to hire a lawyer, one will be appointed to represent you before questioning, if you wish.
You can decide at any time to exercise these rights and not answer any questions or make any statements.

If an individual understands these rights, he knows that the police are adverse to his interests and that any statements made could jeopardize his liberty. He should know that he could remain silent without suffering any consequences; police questioning need not be faced alone and isolated, but instead can be done with the help and presence of an attorney.

The Deaf People among Us

The Deaf people among us are Americans, contributing to our society each day through their work, creativity, devotion to their children, help for those less fortunate, and so forth. As vibrant and productive members of our national community, as citizens of this country, and as human beings, Deaf individuals deserve no less than the full spectrum of freedoms and protections guaranteed all Americans. This includes the protections guaranteed citizens when they are in the greatest peril of losing their liberty, that is, when they have been arrested and are subjected to police interrogation. As outlined above, the rights of an individual who has been taken into custody and subjected to police interrogation arise from the Fifth and Sixth Amendments. For these rights to have any real meaning, a Deaf or other non-English-speaking defendant must be linguistically present to understand what is being said so that he or she knows what the rights are, how to exercise them, and when to exercise them (Berk-Seligson 1990; Morris 1967). Thus, Deaf and other non-English-speaking defendants must be provided with a competent interpreter to be afforded the same fundamental fairness as English-speaking defendants. The failure to do so deprives Deaf Americans of their life or liberty without the due process guaranteed by the Fifth and Fourteenth Amendments (*U.S. ex rel. Negron v. N.Y.* [1970, 2d Cir], 434 F.2d 386, 389).

In short, the rights guaranteed in the Fifth and Sixth Amendments can only be realized by a Deaf individual if he or she understands the *Miranda* warning and subsequent interrogation. These constitutional rights obviate the need for an interpreter during all criminal proceedings. In 1978, the federal government codified this constitutional right in the Federal Court Interpreters Act (U.S. Public Law 95-539). Many states have since passed similar legislation. Nevertheless, regardless of whether or not a state passes such legislation, the right to an interpreter in federal and state criminal cases is a fundamental right of Deaf and other non-English-speaking defendants, which arises from the Fifth, Sixth, and Fourteenth Amendments.

THE LINGUISTIC LANDSCAPE

Like all of the world's natural human languages, ASL is an engineering marvel, crafted unconsciously by the human minds of its users over hundreds, or perhaps thousands, of years. And, like all human languages, ASL is capable of expressing an infinite number of thoughts by utilizing a finite set of rules and meaningful units.

But, despite functional similarities between ASL and other human languages, a basic structural difference is highly relevant to this study. Specifically, visual signals known as nonmanual signals, which co-occur with the articulation of signs, comprise an integral component of the syntax of ASL. They are crucial to comprehensibility and fluency. But production of these signals in a manner that is syntactically correct is one of the most difficult components for second-language learners of ASL to master. Consequently, these signals are often lacking or used ungrammatically in the signed output of interpreters.

A Crucial Difference: The Co-Occurrence of Meaning through the Use of Nonmanual Signals

The human apparatus capable of producing and receiving rapid and varied sound signals differs from the apparatus capable of producing and receiving rapid and varied visual signals. For a sound-based language, the mouth is employed for production and the ear for reception. Since humans possess only one mouth, spoken languages are necessarily linear, constructed by producing one meaningful unit after another. Even if a human possessed more than one mouth, the grammar of spoken languages would necessarily remain linear since the ear and auditory nerve are only capable of processing a single unit at a time.

The human apparatus available for producing and receiving a visual-based language is quite different. For producing visual signals, ASL makes use of at least eight articulators: (1) dominant hand for signing; (2) nondominant hand for signing; (3) eye gaze; (4) eyebrow posture; (5) cheek posture; (6) mouth posture; (7) head movement and posture; and (8) shoulder posture. The postures for each of these articulators are very specific to affect the intended syntactic function or lexical meaning. At any given moment in the production of an ASL sentence, one or more of these articulators produce nonmanual signals at the same time the hands are producing manual signals. Thus, unlike spoken languages that can only produce a linear chain of meaningful units, ASL chains together clusters of meaningful and syntactic units.

For receiving visual signals, ASL uses the eyes. Unlike the ear, which is limited to processing one meaningful sound "bit" at a time, the eyes are powerful receptors capable of processing multiple visual bits and their interrelationship simultaneously.

Because ASL uses multiple articulators to simultaneously produce multiple units of meaning, one might assume that it can express thoughts (or "propositional" content) more quickly than spoken languages. But there is one more piece to this engineering puzzle. Signs produced on the hands (the manual signs) require gross motor movement. Words spoken, on the other hand, are articulated using the fine motor movement of the tongue, jaws, and vocal cords. This fine motor movement for articulating a spoken word is much more rapid than the gross motor movement used for producing signs. The cumulative effect is that speech, although limited to a single channel for communication, uses a channel that is quite rapid. ASL uses slower gross motor movement but simultaneously combines multiple units of meaning. The net result is that spoken language and ASL express propositional content at more or less the same rate.

Syntactic Nonmanual Signals

Nonmanual signals are of two types: lexical and syntactic. See both Liddell (1980) and Metzger and Bridges (1996) for detailed descriptions of lexical and syntactic nonmanual signals in ASL. For the purpose of this study, I have chosen to focus on syntactic nonmanuals since such signals are a crucial syntactic component of nearly every ASL utterance. In particular, I have focused on the following syntactic signals (for which there is widespread agreement among linguists, native Deaf signers, and other researchers as to form and function):

1. Affirmation
2. Negation
3. Yes/No Question
4. Wh- Question
5. Conditionals
6. Listing
7. Topicalization
8. Comparative Structure
9. Role Shift

(Liddell 1980, 10–63; Valli and Lucas 1992, 277–84; Bridges and Metzger 1996, 13–20)

AFFIRMATION

Affirmation of a proposition is signaled by head nodding throughout the sentence being affirmed. For example, the proposition *I am going home* would be signed:

Head:	head nodding
Hands:	PRO. 1 ("I") GO HOME

NEGATION

Negation of a proposition is signaled by head shaking throughout the sentence. Thus, the proposition *I'm not going home* would be signed:

Head:	head shaking
Hands:	PRO. 1 ("I") GO HOME

QUESTIONS

ASL distinguishes between two types of questions. A question that simply seeks confirmation of the information contained within it is known as a "Yes/No Question." This is in contrast to a "Wh- Question," which seeks new information from the listener.

A Yes/No Question is formed by raising the eyebrows throughout the entire sentence. Thus, the proposition *Are you quitting?* is signed as follows:

Eyebrows:	raised-------
Hands:	QUIT PRO. 2 ("YOU")

A WH- QUESTION, ON THE OTHER HAND, IS FORMED BY LOWERING THE EYEBROWS THROUGHOUT THE ENTIRE SENTENCE. ACCORDINGLY, THE PROPOSITION *What's your name?* is signed as follows:

Eyebrows:	lowered------
Hands:	YOUR NAME

CONDITIONALS

A conditional relationship between two clauses is signaled in ASL by two constellations of nonmanual signals, one for each clause. During the condition clause, the eyebrows are raised, and the head, upper body, and hands move slightly to the right or the left. During the result clause, the eyebrows, head, upper body, and hands move into a neutral position with the addition of a head nod or headshake. Whether the head is nodded or shook during the result clause depends on whether the result clause is an affirmative or negative clause. Below is an example of a conditional sentence in ASL:

If you're going to quit, then I'm not going to quit.

Body:	lean right --, neutral---
Head:	lean right --, shake-----
Eyebrows:	raised-----, neutral----
Hands:	QUIT PRO. 2 ("YOU"), QUIT PRO. 1 ("I")

LISTING

To signal for the listener that a list of items, phrases, or sentences should be taken as a group of related items and to demarcate one item from another, a listing function is used. In English, this is accomplished by rising intonation at the end of each sentence, phrase, or item in the group with the exception of the final item, which is accompanied by falling intonation. In ASL, it is accomplished by leaning the upper body forward at the end of each sentence, phrase, or item. For example, the proposition *Can you buy milk, bread, and twelve cookies?* is signed as follows:

Upper Body:	lean lean	lean
Eyebrows:	raised	
Hands:	CAN BUY MILK EGG TWELVE COOKIE	

TOPICALIZATION

Topic-comment structure is the notion of placing a topic first and then commenting on it. ASL uses this structure to place focus on something of heightened importance in an ongoing discourse. Consider the following stretch of English discourse:

> *I don't really care for a lot of meat. Like, I don't like steak or pork or even chicken. But I like **liver**. Really, I do! With onions and green peppers, it's really tasty. I take it you don't like liver?*

In this stretch of discourse, a native English speaker would likely have placed emphatic stress on the word *liver*. In ASL, the same focus can be accomplished by a topic-comment structure. Diagrammed, the sentence would be as follows:

Eye Gaze:	to dom. hand---,neutral ----
Eyebrows:	raised --------,neutral ------
Head:	back and tilt----,nod_---------
Hands:	LIVER PRO. 1 ("I") LIKE, PRO. 1 ("I")

Topic-comment structure for this sentence requires a change in the word order. The basic word order of ASL is subject/verb/object (SVO), but to create the required focus, LIVER would be signed first, followed by the subject and verb. The nonmanual signals accompanying this topic portion of the sentence would be: head tilt back and slightly tilted away from the dominant hand, eyebrows raised, and eye gaze toward the dominant hand. There would then be a pause. For the remaining comment portion of the sentence, the head, eyebrows, and eye gaze return to a neutral position.

It should be noted that subjects and verb phrases might also be topicalized. If the subject is topicalized, no change in word order is necessary. To topicalize a verb phrase, the word order would be verb/object/subject; however, regardless of which syntactic category is topicalized, the nonmanual signals remain the same.

COMPARATIVE STRUCTURE

To compare and contrast in ASL, the signing space in front of the signer is visually divided into two segments—the right half of the signing space and the left half of the space. An item to be compared or contrasted is placed in its own space to the right or left. This is done by leaning the head, upper body, and hands toward one side as the item is introduced into the discourse. Any subsequent comparative or contrastive discourse relating to that item is signaled by leaning the upper body to the respective side and forming the signs in that area. Thus, as a signer moves through comparative or contrastive characteristics of two items, he or she moves the upper body and signs back and forth between the respective sides. The result is a visually iconic diagram of the comparison and contrast. In addition, the signer can efficiently relate discourse to either item without constantly restating the item as the subject of the relevant sentences.

The Crucial Role of Nonmanual Signals in Accurate Interpreting

In this study, the signed interpretations of the subject interpreters were analyzed for their use of the syntactic nonmanual signals described above. ASL utilizes many more nonmanual signals—lexical and syntactic—than those described. Bridges and Metzger (1996), for example, describe and illustrate several other nonmanual signals. But the description above of the limited set of nonmanual signals relevant to this study provides insight into the pivotal role they play in the grammatical mechanics of ASL. As mentioned, these signals tell the listener how a grouping of signs should be taken—as a question, a negated statement, a conditional, and so forth. Moreover, because nonmanual signals can cluster together and co-occur with manual signs, they provide an economy, which results in the production of propositions in ASL at more or less the same speed as spoken languages.

Unfortunately, nonmanual signals are lacking to varying degrees in the signed output of second-language learners of ASL. A lack of this syntactic information can be catastrophic to the Deaf individual's attempt to discern meaning from an interpreter's signed output, which is somewhat akin to a hearing person trying to make sense of the indecipherable word salads of schizophrenics. In addition, an interpreter who lacks the time efficiency of combining nonmanual signals with manual signs will fall behind the English speaker who is turning out propositions at a faster rate. The interpreter who falls behind must catch up, either by deleting information (to the detriment of the Deaf individual's understanding) or by interrupting the speaker to gain more time. In legal settings, interpreters rarely feel they have the standing to repeatedly interrupt police, judges, or lawyers in order to complete their interpretations. Consequently, information deletion is the unfortunate norm.

THE STUDY

This study explores the relationship of interpreting skill to the comprehensibility of signed interpretations of the *Miranda* rights and interrogation. Three approaches were used to explore this issue. First, signed interpretations of the *Miranda* warning and an interrogation were analyzed to determine the frequency of certain syntactic nonmanual signals and the number of lexical items that were signed. Second, the signed interpretations were viewed by ten native Deaf signers. Each Deaf individual was asked to give his or her judgment as to comprehensibility. Third, ethnographic means were used to investigate a case where a Deaf man was charged with rape to determine how the interpreter's skill level affected his understanding of the *Miranda* warning and the subsequent interrogation. In addition, ethnographic interviews of interpreters and lawyers representing Deaf clients in the Cincinnati area explored common police practices for "processing" Deaf suspects who have been arrested.

QUANTITATIVE ANALYSIS OF NONMANUAL SIGNALS AND NUMBER OF WORDS SIGNED

Method

The *Miranda* warning and an interrogation were interpreted by interpreters at varying levels of skill. Their signed output was then analyzed to determine the frequency of certain syntactic nonmanual signals and the number of lexical items (i.e., words) produced. Below, I describe the methods of choosing subjects, data collection, and data analysis.

S U B J E C T S

Participating in this study were nine interpreters at various interpreting skill levels: beginning, intermediate and advanced. Each skill level group was composed of three interpreters.

The beginning interpreters were college students nearing completion of their second ASL course at an accredited interpreter training program. The students who participated in the study were randomly selected from the class roster. The subjects had a hearing instructor for their first course and a Deaf teacher for their second course. *Signing Naturally, Level I* by Vista was the curriculum used for both of their sign courses.

The intermediate interpreters were also college students in an interpreter training program. They had completed at least eight five-credit-hour ASL-interpreting college courses. The subjects were randomly selected from a roster of all students enrolled in a yearlong interpreting practicum course.

The advanced interpreters—two holding full Registry of Interpreters for the Deaf (RID) and National Association of the Deaf (NAD) certifications and one who was also the oldest son of Deaf parents—were selected from the Cincinnati area on the basis of their credentials. One of the certified interpreters had no experience interpreting in legal settings. The other certified interpreter had a moderate amount of experience interpreting in legal settings. The interpreter with Deaf parents had extensive experience interpreting in legal settings.

DATA COLLECTION

The interpreters were asked to interpret the spoken discourse played for them from an audiotape. The audiotape discourse was composed of the five stretches of discourse that are charted in figure 1.

Each section of the audiotape included a brief description of the upcoming stretch of discourse. The description included the setting for the discourse (e.g., witness oath, an interrogation, etc.) and the participants (e.g., lawyer, person suspected of entering country illegally, etc.). The subjects were not told which stretches of discourse would be the focus of the study.

Of the five stretches of discourse, only the *Miranda* warning (section C) and the interrogation (section E) were analyzed. A transcript of section C (the *Miranda* warning) and section E (the interrogation) are set forth in Appendices B and C of this paper. The text for section E was based on an actual interrogation of a defendant by a lawyer, which was related in *The Bilingual Courtroom* by Susan Berk-Seligson. Two actors performed the interrogation on the audiotape—one taking the role of the lawyer and the other taking the role of the defendant.

The room monitor took each subject into a room for videotaping. Each subject was told to interpret, to the best of his or her ability, the five sections of discourse they were about to hear on the audiotape. Each subject was then left alone to interpret. The interpretations were all cold, that is, subjects could not stop the audio- or videotape or repeat any portion of either.

DATA ANALYSIS

The signed interpretations of the *Miranda* warning and the interrogation were analyzed for two linguistic elements deemed crucial to comprehensibility: (1) number of appropriate lexical items; and (2) fre-

Section	Topic	Duration
A	Warm-up narrative—farm story	five minutes
B	Swearing in and perjury penalty—"Do you swear to tell the truth . . ."	thirty seconds
C	*Miranda* warning	one minute
D	Defense closing argument excerpt of Louise Woodward "nanny" trial	five minutes
E	Interrogation of Robert Lopez	three minutes

FIGURE 1. *The five stretches of discourse from the audiotape*

quency of syntactic nonmanual signals. All data analysis was performed by the same analyst, myself, eliminating the skew that can arise from subjective differences between multiple analysts.

The number of appropriate lexical items refers to the number of correct words for each stretch of discourse. Two characteristics of lexical items are important to analyzing the number of correct words in a stretch of discourse. First, what is a word? Second, should lexical nonmanual signals counted as words?

The concept of a word in ASL is somewhat similar to that of English. In English, a word such as *refried* (as in *refried beans*) is a single word even though it is composed of two meaningful units: *re-* and *fried*. In linguistic terms, it is a morphologically complex word composed of two morphemes. Although it is composed of two meaningful units, native English speakers nonetheless recognize it as a single word.

Likewise, ASL has words, some that are morphologically complex and some that are morphologically simple. For example, the concept of *against you* is signed in ASL using a single sign that is morphologically complex. Part of the sign indicates the verb *to be against,* and the other part of the sign indicates the object of the sign, that is, *you.* Although morphologically complex, it is nonetheless recognized as a single sign by native ASL signers. Accordingly, morphologically complex words were counted as single lexical items. In addition, fingerspelled items such as M-E-X-I-C-O were counted as a single word.

The next question is whether lexical nonmanual signals should be counted as words. As already discussed, whereas many nonmanual signals in ASL are syntactic, many carry lexical meaning (e.g., *careless, small, recently,* etc.). These are part of the lexicon (or vocabulary) of ASL. For the purpose of this study, however, word counts were limited to manual signs (signs formed with the hands) to achieve clear comparisons between interpreters. But, it is recognized that the word counts for each interpreter might change slightly if lexical signals were also included in the word counts.

A word count was calculated for each interpretation of the two stretches of discourse—the *Miranda* warning and the interrogation. From these individual counts, average word counts by skill level group were also calculated for both.

The second factor analyzed was the frequency of syntactic nonmanual signals. The signed interpretations were analyzed for the frequency of the following syntactic signals:

1. Affirmation
2. Negation
3. Yes/No Question
4. Wh- Question
5. Conditionals
6. Listing
7. Topicalization
8. Comparative Structure
9. Role Shift

The specific facial, head, and body postures necessary for articulating each of these nonmanual signals were previously described.

The interpreted output was analyzed separately for each of the syntactic nonmanual signals. For example, an interpreted discourse would be analyzed repeatedly and solely for the occurrence of affirmation before it would be analyzed for another syntactic nonmanual signal.

One point relevant to the analysis of syntactic nonmanual signals deserves mention. Many of the nonmanual signals require that the requisite postures of the face, head, or upper body be maintained for an entire clause or sentence. Thus, a syntactic nonmanual signal must be articulated correctly both in terms of facial posture and duration. Both had to be present to be counted as an occurrence of a nonmanual signal. Aborted attempts at forming a syntactic signal were not counted.

Findings and Discussion

The analysis of both the number of lexical items and the frequency of syntactic nonmanual signals revealed dramatic similarities among interpreters of the same skill level (within the group) and dramatic differences between interpreters of different skill levels (between groups).

NUMBER OF LEXICAL ITEMS PRODUCED

With regard to the number of lexical items signed, the beginner interpreters signed an average of only four lexical items during the entire reading of the *Miranda* warning. The intermediate interpreters produced more than nine-fold the number of lexical items for the same stretch of discourse, averaging thirty-eight lexical items. The advanced interpreters produced an average of fifty-two lexical items, a 73 percent increase over the intermediates and a thirteen-fold increase over the beginners.

Equally striking is the consistency within each group. The range of lexical items produced by the subjects of each group was extremely narrow: The beginner group ranged between two and seven lexical items, intermediates ranged between thirty-five and thirty-nine, and advanced interpreters ranged between forty-nine and fifty-five.

The number of lexical items for each interpreter and the average for each group are displayed in table 1.

Table 1 illustrates that the number of lexical items produced increased dramatically as interpreting skill level increased for both the *Miranda* warning and the interrogation. The intermediate group average of 117 was approximately a four-fold increase over the beginner interpreters' group average of 31. The advanced interpreters' group average of 168.6 was over a five-fold increase over the beginners and a nearly 70 percent increase over the intermediates. And again, there was remarkable consistency within each group.

These findings demonstrate dramatic differences in lexical output based on interpreter skill level. During the *Miranda* warning and the

TABLE 1. *Number of Appropriate Lexical Items*

	Miranda Warning	Interrogation
Beginner Signers/Interpreters		
1	3	12
2	2	36
3	7	45
Group Average	4	31
Intermediate Interpreters		
1	35	115
2	40	125
3	39	111
Group Average	38	117
Advanced Interpreters		
1	55	147
2	49	170
3	52	189
Group Average	52	168.6

interrogation, advanced interpreters produced nine times and five times more words respectively than did their beginner counterparts. Moreover, the advanced interpreters produced 70 percent and 73 percent more meaning than even the intermediate interpreters. I would suggest that omitting 70 to 73 percent of the words contained in either the *Miranda* warning or the interrogation might render them incomprehensible to the Deaf defendant.

NUMBER OF SYNTACTIC NONMANUAL SIGNALS PRODUCED

The production of syntactic nonmanual signals also closely correlated with skill level, and, again, the differences between skill level groups were quite striking. Table 2 displays, by skill level, the average number of occurrences of each nonmanual signal. The average of the total number of nonmanual signals produced by each skill level group is also shown. (For the frequency of each nonmanual signal by each interpreter, please see the individual subject score sheets set forth in Appendix D.)

The findings displayed above indicate that the beginner interpreters produced no syntactic nonmanual signals during their interpretation of the *Miranda* warning and a negligible number during their interpretation of the interrogation. Thus, the beginner interpreters produced very few lexical items and even fewer nonmanual signals.

The intermediate interpreters articulated an average of 2.66 syntactic nonmanual signals during the *Miranda* warning and 57 during the interrogation. The advanced interpreters, however, articulated 6.33 and 76 respectively, an increase over the intermediates of nearly two-and-a-half times during the *Miranda* warning and a 75 percent increase during the interrogation. Thus, although the intermediate interpreters successfully articulated a great deal more syntactic signals than the beginners, their signed interpretations lacked a significant amount of syntactic information when compared with the advanced interpreters.

Knowing whether a proposition is a statement or a question, a negative statement or an affirmative statement, a hypothetical or a command, etc., affects one's comprehension of what is being said, and the syntactic signals lacking in the interpretations of the intermediate interpreters had a profound impact on comprehensibility. Consider the difference in meaning if a proposition is not properly negated.

You cannot afford an attorney. vs. *You can afford an attorney.*

TABLE 2. *Frequency of Appropriate Nonmanual Signals*

	Miranda Warning	Interrogation
Beginner Signers/Interpreters' Group Averages		
Affirmation	0	0.33
Negation	0	1.33
Yes/No question	0	0
Wh- question	0	0.66
Conditionals	0	0
Listing	0	0
Topicalization	0	0
Comparative structure	0	0
Role shift	0	3.33
Totals	0	5.65
Intermediate Interpreters' Group Averages		
Affirmation	0.33	3.33
Negation	1	4.66
Yes/No question	0	8.66
Wh- question	0	2
Conditionals	1.33	0
Listing	0	0.33
Topicalization	0	0
Comparative structure	0	0
Role shift	0	38
Totals	1.66	56.98
Advanced Interpreters' Group Averages		
Affirmation	1.66	5
Negation	1.33	7
Yes/No question	0	10.66
Wh- question	0	9.33
Conditionals	2	0
Listing	1	0
Topicalization	0	2.33
Comparative structure	1	0
Role shift	0	41.66
Totals	6.99	75.98

Similarly, consider the effect on meaning if the conditional nonmanual signal is not articulated:

> *If you cannot afford an attorney, one will be appointed for you at government expense.*
>
> vs.
>
> *You cannot afford an attorney. One will be appointed for you at government expense.*

The proposition without the conditional marking leads a defendant to believe that a determination has already been made of his or her indigent status and that the appointment of an attorney is in progress. In reality, an indigent Deaf defendant must assert his desire to speak with an attorney before such a process is initiated. But, unmarked for their conditional relationship, the propositions will lead the Deaf defendant to believe that he or she only need to wait quietly for an appointed attorney to appear.

The results here indicate striking differences in the linguistic output of interpreters based on skill level—both in terms of the number of lexical items and the number of nonmanual signals. I have suggested that the syntactic and lexical deficits in the signed outputs of the beginner and intermediate interpreters have a profound impact on comprehensibility.

NATIVE JUDGMENTS OF COMPREHENSIBILITY

Method

The number of lexical items and syntactic nonmanual signals in the signed interpretations were analyzed because they were deemed to be crucial to the comprehensibility of the signed output. As reasonable as it may seem to assume that the frequency of appropriate lexical items and the frequency of syntactic nonmanual signals are correlates of comprehensibility, it is nonetheless an assumption. Therefore, the signed interpretations were submitted to native ASL users for their judgments of comprehensibility.

SUBJECTS

A total of ten subjects provided comprehensibility judgments. Each of the subjects was a native signer of ASL. A native signer is a Deaf individual who acquired ASL as their first language prior to the age of seven. All of the Deaf subjects use ASL as their primary means of communication. Other social characteristics of the ten subjects are set forth in the table 3.

The social characteristic *Institution* refers to whether a subject had attended a Deaf boarding school for their primary and secondary educations. Except for the small minority of Deaf individuals who have Deaf parents, Deaf boarding schools are the primary loci of ASL acquisition for native signers. To ensure only native signers provided comprehensibility judgments, the subject judges in this study were limited to individuals who had attended such Deaf institutions.

DATA COLLECTION AND ANALYSIS

The signed interpretations were recorded onto videotape in random order. Only the signed interpretations of the *Miranda* warning and the interrogation were included. An instruction in ASL followed each signed interpretation instructing the subject to stop the video and record his or her judgments regarding comprehensibility onto the accompanying score sheet. In addition, because Deaf individuals' command of English is variable, the signed instructions on the video also explained the scores set forth in English on the accompanying score sheet.

The score sheet asked judges to rate each signed interpretation on a scale of 1–4, with 1 being the least comprehensible. Figure 2 shows the scoring system and labels used on the scoring sheet:

Prior to viewing the videotape, subjects were told in ASL that they were participating in a research project relating to courtroom interpreting. Deaf subjects were told that they would be asked for their "overall

TABLE 3. *Sociolinguistic Characteristics of Deaf Subjects*

Subject	Age	Sex	Deaf Parents	Deaf Siblings	Race	Education
1	20	M	No	No	Black	Institution
2	60	F	No	Yes	White	Institution
3	61	M	No	Yes	White	Institution
4	35	M	Yes	Yes	White	Institution
5	22	M	No	No	White	Institution
6	20	F	Yes	No	White	Institution
7	42	F	No	No	White	Institution
8	31	F	Yes	Yes	White	Institution
9	33	M	Yes	Yes	White	Institution
10	45	M	No	No	White	Institution

1	2	3	4
Incomprehensible	Confusing	Fairly Clear	Very Clear

FIGURE 2. *Scoring sheet for comprehensibility judgments*

gut reaction" about the comprehensibility of the *Miranda* warning and the interrogation, and that they need not concern themselves with a grammatical analysis of the signed interpretations.

Findings

A tabulation of the comprehensibility judgments again demonstrated dramatic differences in comprehensibility as a function of interpreter skill level. The signed interpretations of all the beginning interpreters were found to be incomprehensible. This included their interpretations of the *Miranda* warning and the interrogation.

Comprehensibility judgments of the intermediate interpreters' signed output varied by the type of discourse. Intermediates' interpretations of the *Miranda* warning were consistently found by the judges to be confusing, with the exception of two judges who found one of the interpretations of the *Miranda* rights to be incomprehensible. Intermediates' interpretations of the interrogation were uniformly found to be confusing. None of the judges found these interpretations to be very clear.

The interpretations of the advanced interpreters were generally found to be fairly clear. With regard to the *Miranda* warning, three of the judges found the signed output to be confusing. The remaining judges found them to be fairly clear. With regard to the interrogation, six of the judges found the advanced interpreters to be fairly clear. Four found them to be very clear.

Like the intermediate interpreters, the advanced interpreters faired slightly better at conveying the content of the interrogation than they did conveying the content of the *Miranda* warning. I would suggest that the slight differences here in comprehensibility might be related to differences between the two pieces of discourse. One difference is that the *Miranda* warning is a written text, which is read to a defendant, whereas the interrogation arose as an oral interaction, which was orally reproduced for this study. Written discourse is more "compact" than spoken discourse, perhaps due to greater planning time and lack of "visibility" (Chafe 1982). It is more compact in that it has fewer repetitions than oral discourse, is denser in meaning, and exhibits a greater number of syntactically complex structures (Kroll 1977; Chafe 1982; Beaman 1993).

Second, conceptually, the *Miranda* warning is much more complex than the "How did Robert Lopez get to the United States?" theme of the interrogation discourse. Consequently, it may be that a basic understanding of how the legal process works is necessary to understanding the *Miranda* warning. Because of decreased access to written information due to the third- and fifth-grade reading abilities of most Deaf individuals and decreased access to spoken information due to deafness, Deaf individuals as a group probably have less understanding than hearing individuals of how the legal system works. This is consistent with findings by Vernon (1978), who examined how well Deaf college students at Gallaudet understood the *Miranda* warning interpreted by RID-certified interpreters. Vernon found that the students possessed less than a full comprehension of their constitutional rights. Similarly, Fant, Smith, Solow, and Witter-Merithew (1992) have discussed a disparity between hearing and deaf individuals' understanding of the criminal process. Therefore, they suggest that an interpretation should include information implicit in the spoken text to increase the likelihood of authentic understanding of one's constitutional rights. This technique is certainly supported by the *Miranda* decision and its progeny, for it was the arrested individual's actual understanding of the Fifth and Sixth Amendment rights that the Supreme Court sought to achieve through the *Miranda* warning, as opposed to a dogmatic adherence to frozen text regardless of understanding.

In summary, the comprehensibility findings further demonstrate that interpreting skill level dramatically affects the comprehensibility of the *Miranda* rights and interrogation. Only the signed interpretations of the advanced interpreters were found to be fairly clear or clear. I would suggest that the interpretations of the beginner and intermediate interpreters—which Deaf subjects found confusing at best—would not produce an authentic understanding of the Fifth and Sixth Amendment rights.

A CASE STUDY OF INTERROGATION OF A DEAF SUSPECT

Method

What follows is an ethnographic description of a criminal case involving the interrogation of a Deaf defendant, which I investigated as it was still unfolding. On October 27, 2000, police arrested a young Deaf man on the suspicion that he had raped a hearing woman. I will refer to him as Jason White. Jason's attorney contacted me a few weeks after the interrogation. At that point, I conducted several interviews with Jason and his attorney. As part of the interviews, I assessed Jason's ASL and English language skills. I obtained and reviewed a transcript of what was spoken (not signed) during the interrogation. I also obtained a *Miranda* waiver form that Jason had signed and reviewed it with him. Finally, because a police officer had attempted to act as Jason's interpreter during the reading of the *Miranda* rights and subsequent interrogation, I obtained and reviewed the teaching materials and syllabus for the beginning ASL course the police officer had taken.

ETHNOGRAPHIC DESCRIPTION AND FINDINGS

What follows is a description of the legal linguistic aspects of the arrest and interrogation of Jason White, who was arrested on October 27, 2000, on the suspicion of having raped his girlfriend.

Jason was born in a small town in southwest Ohio. His parents were hearing. Consequently, Jason's first exposure to ASL occurred when he began attending elementary school. The school provided him with a sign language interpreter. Although he had never seen ASL before, Jason began acquiring the language by watching the interpreter sign. Despite this less-than-optimal language acquisition process—with the student only having access to a second-language learner who interprets only classroom discourse—Jason acquired ability sufficient for him to communicate on a basic level with the interpreters at his school. There were no other Deaf students at his school.

Jason was less successful at gaining competence at English. At the time of his arrest, his reading and writing skills were approximately at a third-grade level, within the norm for most Deaf adults. This is not surprising given that he could not hear English, in contrast to the hearing children who only needed to learn a written form of their native English language and have phonetic cues to help them master the writing system.

Jason had graduated from high school, was nineteen, and was living on his own when the police arrested him on suspicion of rape. He was alone in his apartment when the police suddenly arrived, handcuffed him, and took him to the local police station. Once there, Jason was provided with an interpreter, a police officer who had completed less than ten weeks of a beginning sign language class. The police officer proceeded to interpret the *Miranda* rights. After the interpretation, Jason was provided with a printed waiver form, on which he placed his initials. In English, the form states that by signing the document, the undersigned understands and waives the constitutional rights contained in the *Miranda* warning.

The police then interrogated Jason for several hours. During his interrogation, the police officer interpreter attempted to voice in English what Jason was signing. Out of frustration, Jason tried to communicate with the police by attempting to speak to them while he signed. Jason attempted to understand what the police were saying to him by trying to read the lips of the police officers and to decipher the signs that the signing police officer was attempting to form. At the conclusion of the interrogation, the police officer interpreter wrote a summary of what he believed Jason had said. The summary was tantamount to a confession. Jason was then held in jail, initially unable to post the bond set by the court.

This scenario raises three important questions. Did Jason truly understand his Fifth Amendment right to remain silent and his Sixth Amendment right to consult with an attorney both prior to and during the interrogation? If he understood those rights, did he actually intend to waive them by signing the form? If Jason understood his rights and knowingly waived them, did he really confess to the crime of rape as the interpreting police officer alleged?

I interviewed Jason several times subsequent to his arrest but prior to trial. We used ASL to converse. During those interviews, I focused on Jason's understanding of his interpreter's signing, his understanding of his Fifth and Sixth Amendment rights, and his understanding of the waiver form that he signed. I also assessed Jason's speechreading, reading, and ASL skills. I did not explore anything relating to the allegations against him since this information is irrelevant to whether the *Miranda* rights had been understood.

Talking with Jason, I found him to be confused about what was happening and about the legal process. He was adamant about one thing, however: He had not raped anyone. Why then did he waive his rights and allegedly confess?

In terms of understanding his rights, Jason told me that the interpreting police officer did not know how to sign and that speechreading did not increase his understanding. Jason did not know that he did not have to speak to the police or that he had a right to talk with an attorney before they asked him questions. Only during our interview, in which we reviewed the *Miranda* waiver form together, did he understand the meaning of his constitutional rights. The fact that Jason could not understand his rights by means of speechreading is unsurprising given the poor speechreading ability he displayed during my language assessment. While Jason could speechread *Hi, how are you?* and other phrases predictable by the context, his ability to speechread unfamiliar material averaged just one in twenty-five words.

Even if he had understood his rights, did he understand that he was waiving them by initialing the form? He initialed the form, he told me, because he thought it indicated that the police officer was excusing him. For Jason, *waiver* meant that he had been excused. The *Miranda* waiver form used is similar to what is used in many jurisdictions. (See Appendix A for the complete waiver form.) The fact that Jason did not understand the form is not surprising. According to my assessment, he possessed, at best, a third-grade reading ability.

The transcript of the interrogation prepared by the police department is quite telling of the kind of communication that occurred. The police department secretary typed everything she could understand. Unintelligible speech was marked by semicolons. Typical of the entire transcript is the following passage in which Detective Hickey is asking Jason where something occurred.

Dt. Hickey: She said what?
Jason: ;;;; ;;;;; ;;;;;;; ;;;;;;;;
Dt. Hickey: Bull shit
Jason: ;;;;; ;;;;; ;;;;;;;; ;;;;;;;;; ;;;;;;;;; ;;;;;;;;; ;;;;;;;;; ;;;;;;;;; ;;;;;;;;; ;;;;;;;;
    ;;;;;;;;; ;;;;;;;;;
Dt. Hickey: Where, where did this happen where did this happen
Jason: ;;;;;;; ;;;;;;;
Dt. Hickey: happen
Jason: ;;;;; ;;;;;;;;;
Dt. Hickey: Yeah location
Jason: ;;; ;;;;;; ;;;;; ;;;;; ;;;;;;; ;;;;
Dt. Hickey: Main Street
Jason: ;;;;;; ;;;;; ;;;;;
Dt. Hickey: Bridge
Jason: ;;;;;; ;;;;;;;;;; ;;;;;

Dt. Hickey: OK The

Jason: ;;;;;;;;;; ;;;;;;; ;;;;;;;;

Dt. Hickey: Second Street Bridge

Jason: ;;; ;;;;;; ;;;;;;;;;;; ;;;;;;;; ;;;;;;;;;

Dt. Hickey: The Lion Bridge

Jason: ;;;;; ;;;;;;;;

Dt. Hickey: OK

The communication difficulty between Detective Hickey and Jason is apparent. Something as simple and concrete as a location required numerous turns. Moreover, none of Jason's speech was comprehensible. Nor did the interpreting officer voice anything Jason signed. In fact, throughout the thirty-one pages of transcript, all of Jason's utterances were encoded as incomprehensible. And the interpreting officer only voiced one statement on behalf of Jason, which was "Just pavement."

Unfortunately, Jason White's experience is not the exception in Ohio. Ethnographic interviews with area attorneys who have represented Deaf clients arrested on criminal charges, Deaf Cincinnatians, and interpreters in the Cincinnati area indicate that Jason's experience is unfortunately the norm in Cincinnati. Police officers who are not trained as interpreters and who hold no interpreting certification typically interpret the *Miranda* warning and interrogation of Deaf suspects. The consequence is that Deaf individuals in the Cincinnati area, by not being informed, are denied their constitutional right to remain silent and their right to counsel. The resulting confusion and duress render these Deaf Americans susceptible to signing waivers that they do not understand, which waive rights that they do not know they have. But, for a judge or jury, the Deaf person's name or initials on the bottom line makes a waiver damning evidence.

It is doubtful that the trampling of Deaf Americans' constitutional rights in this manner is unique to these two jurisdictions. But, trampled they will be until judges, who ultimately control police practices by virtue of excluding tainted evidence, begin to think about the effect of interpreter skill level on the ability to interpret linguistically complex information.

ACKNOWLEDGMENTS

I would like to acknowledge the patience and support of Ceil Lucas. I thank the Deaf and hearing subjects who gave their valuable time to this study. And I thank three Deaf individuals who have given me so much—Joyce Fields Leary, Brent Allen Hull, and Eleanor Elizabeth Hoopes.

REFERENCES

Beaman, K. 1993. Coordination and subordination revisited: Syntactic complexity in spoken and written narrative discourse. In *Coherence in spoken and written discourse*, ed. D. Tannen. Norwood, N.J.: Ablex.

Berk-Seligson, S. 1990. *The bilingual courtroom: Court interpreters in the judicial process.* Chicago: University of Chicago Press.

Bridges, B., and M. Metzger. 1996. DEAF TEND YOUR: *Nonmanual signals in ASL.* Silver Spring, Md.: Calliope Press.

Chafe, W. 1982. Integration and involvement in speaking, writing, and oral literature. In *Spoken and written language: Exploring orality and literacy*, ed. D. Tannen, 35–53. Norwood, N.J.: Ablex.

Fant, L., T. Smith, S. N. Solow, and A. Witter-Merithew. 1992. *Interpreting the Miranda warnings.* Burtonsville, Md.: Sign Media. Videotape.

Levi, J., and A. N. Walker. 1990. *Language in the judicial process.* New York: Plenum Press.

Liddell, S. 1980. *American Sign Language syntax.* The Hague, Netherlands: Mouton.

Padden, C., and T. Humphries. 1989. *Deaf in America: Voices from a culture.* Cambridge, Mass.: Harvard University Press.

Sahakian, W. S. 1968. *History of philosophy.* New York: Barnes and Noble.

Valli, C., and C. Lucas. 1992. *Linguistics of American Sign Language: A resource text for ASL users.* Washington, D.C.: Gallaudet University Press.

Van Cleve, J. V., and B. Crouch. 1989. *A place of their own: Creating the Deaf community in America.* Washington, D.C.: Gallaudet University Press.

Vernon, M., and J. Coley. 1978. Violation of the constitutional rights: The language impaired person and the *Miranda* warnings. *Journal of Rehabilitation of the Deaf* 11(4): 1–9.

Miranda Waiver Form

Miranda Warning

I am a Police Officer for the City of Franklin, Warren County, Ohio. I must advise you of your Constitutional Rights before you are asked any questions.

WARNING

#1.   You have the right to remain silent.

        Do you understand? Yes_____ No_____

#2.   Anything you say can and will be used against you in a court of law.

        Do you understand? Yes_____ No_____

#3.   You have the right to talk to a lawyer and have him present with you while you are being questioned.

        Do you understand? Yes_____ No_____

#4.   If you cannot afford to hire a lawyer, one will be appointed to represent you before questioning, if you wish.

        Do you understand? Yes_____ No_____

#5.   You can decide at any time to exercise these rights and not answer any questions or make any statements.

        Do you understand? Yes_____ No_____

Interviewee Signature_____

Date and Time_____

WAIVER OF CONSTITUTIONAL RIGHTS

I have read this statement of my rights and I fully understand what my rights are. I do not want a lawyer at this time. I understand and know what I am doing. No promises of any kind, hope of reward, favors or threats have been made to me. Upon being advised of my Constitutional Rights I wish to make the following verbal and/or written statement without my attorney being present. I declare that I knowingly, voluntarily, and intelligently waive my Constitutional Rights.

Interviewee Signature_____

Officer Signature_____

Witness_____

Witness_____

Text of Section C of Audiotape: *Miranda* **Warning**

[The following is a transcript of section C portion of the audiotape, the portion which includes the *Miranda* warning. Below is the complete transcript of this section, including the brief introduction given to the subject interpreter.]

The next section is section C.
The setting for this will be at a police station.
The purpose of it will be to obtain a statement from the defendant who has been arrested.
And prior to that time, his rights will be read to him. And when you begin to hear me speak again, you can begin to interpret.

You have the right to remain silent.
Anything you say can and will be used against you in a court of law.
You have the right to consult with an attorney before questioning.
You have the right to have your attorney present with you during questioning.
If you cannot afford an attorney, one will be appointed for you at government expense.
You may choose to exercise these rights at any time.

Here ends section B.

Text of Section C of Audiotape:
Interrogation of Robert Lopez

[The following is a transcript of section E portion of the audiotape, a cross-examination of a defendant by an attorney. Below is a complete transcript of this section, including the brief introduction given to the subject interpreter.]

Ok, section E, which is the final section, is going to be umm the questioning by a prosecuting attorney of a witness.
The witness' name is Robert Lopez, um the issue that they are talking about is whether Robert Lopez entered the United States illegally.
So that is what the questioning we'll be focusing upon.
Um.. so in just a few minutes, you will begin to interpret when you begin to hear me speak again.

ATTORNEY: *Sir, would you state your name please.*
DEFENDANT: *Robert Lopez.*
ATTORNEY: *How old are you?*
DEFENDANT: *I am twenty-six years old.*
ATTORNEY: *Have you ever used any other name?*
DEFENDANT: *No sir.*
ATTORNEY: *Where were you born?*
DEFENDANT: *In Mexico City.*
ATTORNEY: *And of what country are you a citizen?*
DEFENDANT: *Um . . . I don't understand.*
ATTORNEY: *Of what country are you a citizen?*
DEFENDANT: *Uh . . . Mexico.*
ATTORNEY: *I call your attention to the evening of March 23rd and the morning of March 24th.*
Were you in the United States at that time?
DEFENDANT: *Um . . . March 24th?*
ATTORNEY: *Yes.*
DEFENDANT: *No sir.*
ATTORNEY: *Do you recall entering the United States during the month of March at all?*
DEFENDANT: *No.*

ATTORNEY: *When did you last enter the country?*

DEFENDANT: *This is the very first time.*

ATTORNEY: *When was that sir?*

DEFENDANT: *I don't remember, I think it was around the 22nd.*

ATTORNEY: *Did you have any papers or documents to offer as your entry?*

DEFENDANT: *No sir.*

ATTORNEY: *Were you inspected by immigration officers when you entered the United States?*

DEFENDANT: *Um . . . "inspection" . . . "inspected" . . . I don't understand what you mean by . . . "inspected."*

ATTORNEY: *Did you enter through a point of entry?*

DEFENDANT: *No sir.*

ATTORNEY: *Did you enter illegally?*

DEFENDANT: *Yes.*

ATTORNEY: *Would you explain for the court the circumstances surrounding that entry?*

DEFENDANT: *Um . . . yes . . . well, you mean the way I came in?*

ATTORNEY: *Yes sir, did you cross through a fence or . . . ?*

DEFENDANT: *Yes, through a fence.*

ATTORNEY: *Had you made any arrangements for a ride before you left Mexico?*

DEFENDANT: *Yes sir.*

ATTORNEY: *How did that come about?*

DEFENDANT: *Well, since I didn't have any money, I ah asked for a ride.*

ATTORNEY: *Who did you ask?*

DEFENDANT: *Mr. Humberto.*

ATTORNEY: *Mr. Humberto?*

DEFENDANT: *Yes sir.*

ATTORNEY: *Do you see Mr. Humberto in the courtroom here now?*

Here ends the final section. Thank you very much.

[The cross-examination above is based on a cross-examination interpreted into Spanish that was analyzed in *The Bilingual Courtroom* (1990) by Susan Berk-Seligson.]

Frequency of Nonmanual Signals by Each Subject

MIRANDA WARNING INTERROGATION

Beginner Signers/Interpreters

INTERPRETER A

Affirmation	o	o
Negation	o	1
Yes/No Question	o	o
Wh- Question	o	o
Conditionals	o	o
Listing	o	o
Topicalization	o	o
Comparative Structure	o	o
Role Shift	o	o
TOTAL	o	1

INTERPRETER B

Affirmation	o	o
Negation	o	o
Yes/No Question	o	o
Wh- Question	o	o
Conditionals	o	o
Listing	o	o
Topicalization	o	o
Comparative Structure	o	o
Role Shift	o	o
TOTAL	o	o

INTERPRETER C

Affirmation	o	1
Negation	o	3
Yes/No Question	o	o
Wh- Question	o	2
Conditionals	o	o
Listing	o	o

Topicalization	o	o
Comparative Structure	o	o
Role Shift	o	10
TOTAL	o	**16**

Beginner Interpreters'/Signers' Group Averages

Affirmation	o	.33
Negation	o	1.33
Yes/No Question	o	o
Wh- Question	o	.66
Conditionals	o	o
Listing	o	o
Topicalization	o	o
Comparative Structure	o	o
Role Shift	o	3.33
TOTAL	o	**5.65**

Intermediate Interpreters

INTERPRETER A

Affirmation	o	3
Negation	2	4
Yes/No Question	o	10
Wh- Question	o	1
Conditionals	3	o
Listing	o	1
Topicalization	o	o
Comparative Structure	o	o
Role Shift	o	37
TOTAL	5	**56**

INTERPRETER B

Affirmation	1	4
Negation	1	5
Yes/No Question	o	8
Wh- Question	o	2
Conditionals	1	o

Listing	o	o
Topicalization	o	o
Comparative Structure	o	o
Role Shift	o	39
TOTAL	3	58

Affirmation	o	3
Negation	o	5
Yes/No Question	o	8
Wh- Question	o	3
Conditionals	o	o
Listing	o	o
Topicalization	o	o
Comparative Structure	o	o
Role Shift	o	38
TOTAL	o	57

Intermediate Interpreters' Group Averages

Affirmation	.33	3.33
Negation	1	4.66
Yes/No Question	o	8.66
Wh- Question	o	2
Conditionals	1.33	o
Listing	o	.33
Topicalization	o	o
Comparative Structure	o	o
Role Shift	o	38
TOTAL	2.66	56.98

Advanced Interpreters

SIGNER/INTERPRETER A

Affirmation	1	3
Negation	1	6
Yes/No Question	o	12

Wh- Question	0	9
Conditionals	2	0
Listing	1	0
Topicalization	0	2
Comparative Structure	1	0
Role Shift	0	43
TOTAL	**6**	**75**

INTERPRETER B

Affirmation	2	7
Negation	2	8
Yes/No Question	0	10
Wh- Question	0	9
Conditionals	2	0
Listing	1	0
Topicalization	0	1
Comparative Structure	1	0
Role Shift	0	43
TOTAL	**7**	**78**

INTERPRETER C

Affirmation	2	5
Negation	1	7
Yes/No Question	0	10
Wh- Question	0	10
Conditionals	2	0
Listing	1	0
Topicalization	0	4
Comparative Structure	1	0
Role Shift	0	39
TOTAL	**6**	**75**

Advanced Interpreters' Group Averages

Affirmation	1.66	5
Negation	1.33	7
Yes/No Question	0	10.66
Wh- Question	0	9.33
Conditionals	2	0

Listing	1	0
Topicalization	0	2.33
Comparative Structure	1	0
Role Shift	0	41.66
TOTALS	**6.99**	**75.98**

Court Interpreting for Signing Jurors:

Just Transmitting or Interpreting?

Susan Mather and Robert Mather

With the important assistance of sign language interpreters, deaf people who use sign language are participating in jury service with greater frequency. Experience has shown that using an interpreter does not violate the sanctity of the jury system and the secrecy of jury deliberations, and that a deaf juror may analyze evidence as well as a juror who can hear the proceedings.

Certain issues concerning the accuracy of court interpretation, however, continue to emerge. These issues expose a tension between the twin goals of a word-for-word translation of court proceedings and interpreting to provide legal equivalence. As explained in this paper, it is impossible and ineffective for a sign language interpreter to provide literal interpretation by adhering strictly to spoken English. Instead, the interpreter—provided he or she is appropriately trained to work in legal settings—should be allowed to interpret faithfully and accurately only what is stated, without omitting, adding, or altering anything.

These issues have been addressed at some length in the professional literature and in a few reported cases. Yet, they have not been completely resolved. The purpose of this paper is to summarize the results of our review of the case law and literature and make suggestions for courts to effectively cope with these issues, that is, how to ensure the accuracy of court interpretation in sign language.

To put these issues in proper context, we will discuss them in the following order. First, we will provide an overview of the statutory and

Points of view and opinions stated in this paper are those of the authors and do not represent the official position or policies of Gallaudet University or the U.S. Department of Justice.

constitutional rights of people with disabilities who serve on juries and have access to the courts, the statutory provisions for the appointment of court interpreters, and the English literacy requirement for jurors. Second, we will discuss American Sign Language (ASL) and interpretation. Third, we will detail current standards for court interpretation. Fourth, we will discuss some cases reported in the case law and literature that address the roles of court interpreters appointed to ensure effective participation by signing deaf jurors. Included is an examination of a New York case where a court instructed an interpreter to function as a transmitter instead of an interpreter. In our discussion, we will demonstrate why such instructions are inappropriate and restrictive. We will conclude this paper with suggestions for improving the accuracy of court interpretation.

Whereas the focus of this paper is on the use of court interpreters for signing deaf jurors, the principles discussed and the recommendations made can serve as the basis for courts to develop or otherwise review their own sign language policies.

LEGAL BACKGROUND

Access to Courts

STATE AND LOCAL COURTS

Federal Law

Title II of the Americans with Disabilities Act (ADA), enacted in 1990, prohibits discrimination by state and local government agencies and requires them to ensure that all the activities, programs, and services they provide are accessible to people with disabilities. Title II generally applies to state and local governments, including courts, but it does not apply to the federal court system.

Title II prohibits general discrimination against people with disabilities by state and local governments in the areas of program accessibility, communication, and employment. The ADA protects "qualified individuals with a disability" from discrimination on the basis of disability. A "qualified individual with a disability" is defined as an individual with a disability who—with or without the provision of auxiliary aids; removal of architectural, communication, or transportation barriers; or "reasonable" modifications to rules, policies, and practices—meets the essential requirements for the receipt of services or participation in programs or activities provided by a public entity. Beyond this general non-discrimination mandate, Title II contains general and specific prohibitions on discrimination in several areas. We will address only two of the areas that are relevant here: (1) policies, practices, and procedures, and (2) communication.

Title II covers policies, practices, or procedures of state and local governments. Section 35.130(b)(7) of the regulation requires that state and local courts make "reasonable" modifications in policies, practices, or procedures where necessary to avoid discrimination based on disability, unless doing so would result in a fundamental alteration to the program or create undue financial and administrative burdens.

It has been held that the automatic exclusion of a person with a disability from jury duty would violate the ADA. In *Galloway v. Superior Court of the District of Columbia,* Donald Galloway sued the District of Columbia Superior Court, alleging that it violated the law by categorically excluding blind people from jury service. The federal court agreed and ruled that the exclusion of blind people from jury service violated the ADA. The court observed that

> the Superior Court admits persons who are deaf to jury panels and has never suggested that simply because they cannot hear, they cannot serve. In fact, the Superior Court accommodates those individuals by providing sign language interpreters.

The court also stated that the superior court's policy on deaf jurors "evidences a lack of prejudice towards those with hearing impairments and demonstrates [the court's] ability to look behind archaic stereotypes thrust upon disabled persons." Similarly, in a Title II administrative case, the Philadelphia Court of Common Pleas established, as part of a settlement agreement under the ADA, procedures available for prospective jurors with disabilities to obtain reasonable modifications to court policies, practices, and procedures.

As state or local government entities, courts are required under Title II to ensure that their communications with applicants, participants, and members of the public with disabilities are as effective as their communications with other participants, unless doing so would result in a fundamental alteration to the program or create undue financial and administrative burdens. To provide equal access, a public entity is required to make available "appropriate auxiliary aids and services" where necessary to ensure effective communication.

Under Title II, auxiliary aids and services include a wide range of services and devices that promote effective communication. Pertaining to court proceedings, examples of auxiliary aids and services for individuals who are deaf or hard of hearing include qualified interpreters, note takers, computer-aided transcription services, written materials, assistive listening systems, open and closed captioning, videotext displays, and exchange of written notes.

In 1993, the U.S. Department of Justice issued the *Title II Technical Assistance Manual Covering State and Local Government Programs and Services,* which explained in lay terms what state and local governments must do to ensure that their services, programs, and activities are provided to the public in a nondiscriminatory manner. This document explains that the type of auxiliary aid or service necessary to ensure effective communication will vary in accordance with the length and complexity of the communication involved. It also addresses common issues of effective communication in the context of court proceedings.

> Because of the importance of effective communication in State and local court proceedings, special attention must be given to the communications needs of individuals with disabilities involved in such proceedings. Qualified interpreters will usually be necessary to ensure effective communication with parties, jurors, and witnesses who have hearing impairments and use sign language. For individuals with hearing impairments who do not use sign language, other types of auxiliary aids or services, such as assistive listening devices or computer-assisted transcription services, which allow virtually instantaneous transcripts of courtroom argument and testimony to appear on displays, may be required.

In choosing an auxiliary aid or service, primary consideration must be given to a person's choice regarding effective communication. When required, the court must provide an opportunity for individuals with disabilities to request the appropriate auxiliary aids and services and must give primary consideration to the individual's choices. The phrase "primary consideration" means that the court must honor the choice, unless it can demonstrate that another equally effective means of communication is available or that the use of the means chosen would result in a fundamental alteration in the service, program, or activity or create undue financial and administrative burdens.

The manual explains the reason for giving primary consideration to the person's preferred choice as follows:

> It is important to consult with the individual to determine the most appropriate auxiliary aid or service, because the individual with a disability is most familiar with his or her disability and is in the best position to determine what type of aid or service will be effective. Some individuals who were deaf at birth or who lost their hearing before acquiring language, for example, use sign language as their primary form of communication and may be uncomfortable or not proficient with written English, making use of a notepad an ineffective means of communication.
>
> Individuals who lose their hearing later in life, on the other hand, may not be familiar with sign language and can communicate effectively through writing. For these individuals, use of a word processor with a videotext display may provide effective communication in transactions that are long or complex, and computer-assisted simultaneous transcription may be necessary in courtroom proceedings. Individuals with less severe hearing impairments are often able to communicate most effectively with voice amplification provided by an assistive listening device.

Title II defines "qualified interpreter" as one who is able to interpret effectively, accurately, and impartially, using any necessary specialized vocabulary. Appendix A to the regulation explains that the definition

> focuses on the actual ability of the interpreter in a particular interpreting context to facilitate effective communication between the public entity and the individual with disabilities.

The manual explains that the court should provide a qualified interpreter, that is, an interpreter who is able to use the particular sign language system employed by the deaf juror. Thus, to effectively assist signing deaf jurors, qualified sign interpreters are trained in court interpretation as well as legal procedure and terminology.

As will be explained below, current state laws governing court interpreters using sign language virtually require that interpreters be certified. Although the Title II definition of a qualified interpreter does not require that interpreters be "certified," this definition would not necessarily pre-empt all state laws mandating the use of only certified interpreters, as long as a certified interpreter appointed by a court is at least "qualified." Appendix A to Title II states that the rule does not "supersede any re-quirement of state law for use of a certified interpreter in court proceed-ings."

Several state courts have entered into settlement agreements with the U.S. Department of Justice to adopt a policy to provide appropriate aux-iliary aids, including qualified sign language interpreters, to provide ef-fective communication in court proceedings for deaf jurors. For instance, in a 1997 settlement agreement, the Harrison County of Mississippi com-mitted its courts to provide when necessary the appropriate auxiliary aids and services, including qualified interpreters, so that people with a disabilities will have the opportunity to serve as jurors. The county agreed to establish a policy that provided interpreters for individuals serving on jury duty, to notify the public about the policy, and to in-struct district court officials to adhere to it.

In short, to ensure equality of opportunity and effective participation by signing deaf jurors under Title II, state and local courts must adopt a three-pronged approach. First, courts must review and revise their rules, practices, and procedures whenever necessary to provide effective com-munication with a signing deaf juror. Second, court officers should meet with the deaf person to determine the appropriate services or modifica-tions for effective communication prior to jury service. Third, when the court determines that the service of a qualified interpreter is appropriate, it should appoint qualified sign language interpreters who are trained in legal procedure and terminology and interpreting in legal settings. Cru-cial to this approach is that the interpreter be allowed to interpret accu-rately.

State Laws

Whereas most state laws have been enacted to ensure that persons who are deaf have formal access to court or administrative proceedings, with a focus on the provision of certified or qualified court interpreters, some states have explicitly required the provision of interpreting services in cases of deaf jurors.

For instance, the Texas juror statute states that no deaf or hard of hearing person should be disqualified to serve solely because of hearing loss. The statute requires a court to provide auxiliary aids and services, including interpreters, to accommodate deaf jurors in accordance with the ADA. The California Code of Civil Procedure (section 198, subd. [2]) allows individuals with certain disabilities (i.e., loss of sight or hearing in any degree) to be jurors, necessitating the use of interpreters. The Connecticut statute (section 16-1) provides interpreters for deaf or hard of hearing jurors. The Rhode Island Judiciary issued a policy stating that when an individual with a communication disability is serving as a juror, a sign language interpreter or other appropriate auxiliary aid or service should be secured.

FEDERAL COURTS

The Federal Court Interpreters Act governs access to federal courts and provides that in any criminal or civil action initiated by the United States, the judge must use the services of a certified interpreter for a party or witness who is non-English-speaking or has "a hearing impairment." The act does not require the provision of interpreters for non-English-speaking persons who are summoned to serve on the jury; however, it authorizes the trial judge to appoint a sign language interpreter to provide services to a party, witness, or other participant in a judicial proceeding who has a hearing impairment.

The Judicial Conference of the Administrative Office of the United States Courts has established a policy that all federal courts will "provide reasonable accommodations to persons with communications disabilities." Under this policy, the courts will provide, at court expense, sign language interpreters or other appropriate auxiliary aids to persons who are deaf or hard of hearing in court proceedings. This policy, however, does not apply to spectators or to jurors whose qualifications for service are determined under other provisions of law. One of these qualifications to be determined is the English literacy requirement.

English Literacy Requirement for Jury Service

Except for New Mexico, most state juror qualifications statutes exclude from jury service those who are not sufficiently proficient in English to understand proceedings in which they are to participate. New Mexico's constitution (art. 8, sec. 3) protects against the loss of the right to jury service because of an "inability to speak, read, or write the English or Spanish languages" and requires a trial court to make every reasonable effort to accommodate a potential juror for whom language difficulties present a barrier to participation in court proceedings. Under the Federal Jury Act, jurors must be able to speak the English language and read, write, and understand English with sufficient proficiency to satisfactorily complete the juror qualification form.

The requirement to have sufficient knowledge of the English language will not disqualify deaf people who cannot speak English because courts are required to provide an interpreter to interpret spoken English into sign language. For instance, the First Circuit Court explained in *United States v. Morris* that nothing stated in the Federal Jury Act implicitly or explicitly requires that federal jurors deliberate in English. Rather, the First Circuit Court explained that all of the requirements listed by Congress that pertain to federal jurors have to do with the juror's ability to understand the proceedings in court; the statute deals principally with the requirement of qualifications for federal jurors, not with their actions during trial. The court went on, saying:

> Nowhere in the statute are jurors instructed as to what language they must use when deliberating. Furthermore, the legislative history of this statute clearly demonstrates that Congress' principal concern in enacting this statute was that federal jurors meet the constitutional requirement that they represent a fair cross-section of the community from which they were drawn.

The federal district court in *DeLong v. Brumbaugh* held that a Pennsylvania statute, which had a restriction similar to the Federal Jury Act, did not exclude signing deaf people.

Fallahay, in his 2000 report *The Right to a Full Hearing: Improving Access to the Courts for People Who Are Deaf or Hard of Hearing* suggests that the proper inquiry into whether a person meets the English language requirement is whether the person has the ability "to communicate effectively with those who speak English."

SIGN LANGUAGE AND INTERPRETATION

American Sign Language and Contact Signing

ASL, a full and independent language, has a unique syntax and structure pattern and does not correspond with written or spoken English syntax. In terms of syntax, for example, ASL frequently uses a topic-comment syntax, whereas English uses subject-verb-object syntax. ASL has its own morphology (rules for the creation of words), phonetics (rules for handshapes), and grammar, which are very unlike those found in spoken languages.

Facial features such as eyebrow motion and lip or mouth movements are also significant in ASL, as they form a crucial part of the grammatical system. In addition, ASL makes use of the space surrounding the signer to describe places and persons that are not present. As mentioned earlier, it has a very complex grammar. Unlike spoken languages, which only have one serial stream of phonemes, sign languages can have multiple things occurring at the same time.

Within the realm of sign language, *contact signing* refers to a form of signing that results from interactions between people who are deaf and people who can hear. This form of signing is a combination of ASL vocabulary, English word order, and certain other English features (e.g., auxiliary verbs). Contact signing is what was previously referred to as *Pidgin Signed English*. Many in the field of linguistics considered Pidgin Signed English a misnomer. Contact signing is distinct from Signed English, which is a manual representation of English often produced simultaneously with spoken English and with no features of ASL.

Interpreting

Interpreting is the transmission of a spoken or signed message from one language (the source language) to another (the target language) (Frishberg 1990). A sign language interpreter interprets a message expressed in spoken English into ASL or contact signing, and vice versa.

Within the field of sign language interpreting, Frishberg says, there is a process called *transliterating,* during which an interpreter changes a message expressed in spoken English to a manually coded form of the language. In the target language, transliterating retains some source language elements or renders the analyzed message into a sign variety most readily understood (but not necessarily in the same word order as the source message). Factors to be carefully considered in determining whether transliterating should be achievable in a given legal setting include the interpreter's linguistic ability, the speed of the proceedings, and the frequent or infrequent use of legal jargon.

Translation relates to written language. Frishberg explains that translation is converting a written text from one language into written text in another language. As Hewitt (1995) explains, in translation, "[t]he source of the message being converted is always a written language."

COURT INTERPRETATION

Types and Functions of Court Interpreting

Court interpreting can be defined as "oral interpretation of speech from one language to another in a legal setting" (González, Vasquez, and Mikkelson 1991). Court interpreters use two modes of interpreting—simultaneous and consecutive. Simultaneous interpreting is rendering an interpretation at the same time someone is speaking or signing. Consecutive interpreting is rendering an interpretation after the speaker or signer has stopped speaking or signing and prior to production of the next message. This may occur after a few sentences or after the entire presentation.

Hewitt (1995) defines the functions of spoken language court interpreting as proceedings interpreting, witness interpreting, and interview interpreting. Sign language interpreters divide and collapse the functions differently: (1) proceedings interpreting, which includes witness interpreting, and (2) counsel table interpreting (also called defense interpreting, plaintiff interpreting, law office interpreting, and interview interpreting).

Each of these functions relate to the purpose or the setting in which interpreting occurs. Hewitt describes these functions as follows:

> Proceedings interpreting is used in cases of non-English-speaking participants including jurors, in order to make them able to participate effectively during the proceedings. In this function, the interpreter would use the simultaneous mode of interpreting as the preferred mode. What the interpreter interprets is not part of the record of proceedings, except when the interpreter asks the judge for clarifications or when the juror who is deaf asks the judge a question.

Witness interpreting refers to the interpretation that occurs when a witness presents evidence to the court. This interpreting function for non-English-speaking or signing witnesses is performed in the consecutive mode; the English language portions of the interpretation are part of the record of the proceeding. Witness interpreting should be consecutive whether the witness speaks Spanish or is deaf. The function of witness interpreting also applies to communications during arraignments, pleas, or sentence hearings between a judge and a non-English-speaking participant.

Interview interpretation occurs in interviews or consultation settings where the interpreting service is to facilitate communication between attorneys and clients. Interviewing interpretation may be provided in either or both the simultaneous and consecutive modes during an interview, depending on the circumstances. This also includes the function of interpreting lawyer/client conversations in court and monitoring the proceeding interpreters during court proceedings (or at depositions, mediation, and arbitrations).

In short, the function of jury interpreting is essentially the same as that of proceedings interpreting, including communications between the court and the juror.

Standards for Court Interpretation

In its report on the qualifications of court interpreters, the Federal Judicial Center (1989) wrote that the main objective of court interpreting is "to provide legal equivalence." González et al. (1991) explain that to maintain legal equivalence, the interpreter must attempt "to translate with exactitude . . . while accurately reflecting a speaker's nuances and level of formality."

Citing the legislative history of the Court Interpreters Act, one federal court in *United States v. Torres* held that the interpreter's duty is to "translate all statements, without restriction by the court." The court also explained that the interpreter should use the consecutive mode of interpretation, "except in those situations where the court determines, and *all the parties agree,* that the simultaneous or summary mode will aid in the efficient administration of justice." The court also stated that the summary mode of translation would be "used very sparingly." Summary translation is defined as "allowing the interpreter to condense and distill the speech." Roseann González, director of the Federal Court Interpreter Certification Project, and her colleagues write that, to maintain legal equivalence, the interpreter must:

> interpret the original source material without editing, summarizing, deleting, or adding while conserving the language level, style, tone, and intent of the speaker or to render what may be termed the legal equivalence of the source message. (González et al. 1991)

They explain that legal equivalence also requires conservation of speech style.

It is important to remember from the beginnings of judicial proceedings triers of fact (the judge or jury) have to determine the veracity of a witness's message on the basis of an impression conveyed through the speaker's demeanor. The true message is often in how something is said rather than what is said; therefore, the style of a message is as important as its content.

The interpreter is required to render in a verbatim manner the form and content of the linguistic and paralinguistic elements of a discourse, including all of the pauses, hedges, self-corrections, hesitations, and emotion as they are conveyed through tone of voice, word choice, and intonation; this concept is called conservation.

In her paper "Verbatim Interpretation: An Oxymoron," Mikkelson (2000a) states that both the interpreting and legal communities have conflicting expectations regarding the role of court interpreters. She explains that the legal profession expects court interpreters to provide a verbatim interpretation of the proceedings. She further argues that the standards for court interpretation should be defined internally instead, that nearly all experts in the field of the interpreting process have accepted the standards of functional equivalency and meaning-based translation as appropriate, and that the verbatim requirement is "outmoded."

Mikkelson explains that even the statutes and court rules governing court interpretation "tend to emphasize the need to convey meaning rather than adhering strictly to the form of the source-language message." As an example, she cites the California Standards of Judicial Administration, which does not mention the term "verbatim or anything similar." Section 18.1 (8) of the California Standards states, "All words, including slang, vulgarisms, and epithets, should be interpreted to convey the intended meaning."

Mikkelson writes:

Obenaus (1995) points out, "the fact that legal texts require precision and impose restrictions on the translator is all too often misconstrued to mean that they have to be translated literally, leading to unsatisfactory and awkward results." What is really required is that the interpreter account for every word and every other element of meaning in the source-language message. Thus, if a witness answers the source-language equivalent of, "I, well, I don't know . . . I suppose . . . yes,

I think I saw him there," the interpreter's version in English should not simply be "I think I saw him there," but should reflect all of the uncertainty conveyed in the original. As González and her colleagues (1991) note, "The reason for this high standard of accuracy is that the interpreter is the voice of the non-English speaker . . . the words of the interpreter are the only permanent record of what the witness or the defendant said." (2000a)

Accuracy also means giving the receiver the complete message, including the aspects carried by pauses, hesitations, or other silent or nonverbal signals. The interpreter sends the full message, not merely the words. In addition, accuracy means that the interpreter will interpret the entire message, regardless of whether the interpreter finds the content or language distasteful.

THE DEAF JUROR EXPERIENCE

People v. Guzman

The court interpretation endorsement of Signed English for signing jurors first appeared in the 1984 New York Superior Court decision in *People v. Guzman.* In that case, the court found that allowing a deaf person to serve as a juror with an interpreter provided by the court did not violate a defendant's Sixth Amendment rights. At issue was whether a deaf juror, assisted by a sign language interpreter, was able to meet the statutory English requirement to serve on a jury. The defendant assumed that the deaf person was unable to speak English because the interpreter assisted the juror at trial. The court rejected the argument for the following reasons.

First, the court noted that the juror in question spoke, read, and wrote English, but that he was "profoundly deaf." Both the court and he communicated through a court-appointed interpreter using Signed English. The court clarified that when using Signed English, as opposed to ASL, the interpreter functioned as a signer.

For purposes of clarity in this case, the interpreter will be referred to as a signer, since she was not communicating with [the juror], nor he with her, in American Sign Language.

The court stated that ASL is a separate language from English, with its own grammar and syntax. The court also stated that a person who signs with a person using ASL is therefore considered "a translator or interpreter just as any foreign language interpreter serves that function in a court proceeding." The court concluded that since the juror used Signed English, "which is not a separate language—it is English in a different form," the interpreter was not translating or interpreting, but merely transmitting.

> When a person communicates in signed English, the exact words in English are transmitted from the speaker through the signer to the listener, but always in English. This is done by means of hand signals which represent each of the words in English, just as a group of characters typed on a page represents a word in English. The signer can be analogized to a modem, a device which allows one computer to "talk" to another over a transmission line. It allows for transmission between two things which otherwise could not communicate. The word itself is an acronym for modulator-demodulator. The modem transmits or receives a message and passes it on. It does not translate. Another way to look at the signer who uses signed English is as an input/output buffer. This device allows one electronic device to "talk" to another. It is called a buffer because one computer sends at a slightly different rate than the other receives. Again, it is the same language, merely a different form. It is clear that in order for a deaf person to meet the statutory language requirement for jury service that person must understand and communicate in English using either signed English, or lip reading, or finger-spelling or any combination thereof as the mode of communication.

In a footnote, the court indicated that people "who know only American Sign Language and do not know English" would not meet the statutory English requirement any more than would any other non-English-speaking person.

The court observed:

> There is certainly no question that deaf persons are as capable as anyone else of understanding legal jargon or any other technical jargon used by expert witnesses. The deaf are found in many highly technical professions, including medicine, engineering, and the law.

Guzman rejected the defendant's other arguments that interpreting for a deaf person created a likelihood of inaccuracy in translation, that there were subtle nuances of voice that could not be projected through a signer, and that the presence of a signer was disruptive at trial.

With respect to the accuracy of the signer's transmission, the court noted that the issue of accuracy was equally important when any non-English-speaking witness or defendant testifies through an interpreter. The court stated that the jury, judge, attorneys, court reporter, and all future appellate courts are dependent on the record made by that interpreter. The court stated, "If we do not trust the skills of that person then we have no trial at all" and further commented that court administrators should define qualifications and impose standards for interpreters.

Regarding the issue of the loss of subtle nuances of vocal inflection, the court explained, "Any such nuances are always open to interpretation." The court added:

> In reality, no juror, whether hearing or deaf, hears everything that should be heard, interprets everything as it is meant to be interpreted, processes everything in the same fashion or reaches a decision in the same way. Some jurors are better educated than others, some are more observant, some more aware of auditory cues and some unfortunately hear and understand little or nothing that has gone on in the proceedings.

The court said that a

> qualified signer can express the speaker's intonation, inflection, syntax and other variations of speech through a combination of facial expressions and movements. These expressions and movements are not a commentary on the state of mind of the declarant but are indications of such things as pauses, modulations of voice and the speed of the declarant's speech.

The court concluded, "The blunt constraint that no deaf person can be qualified to sit as a juror is a passé conclusion which defies and has no connection with reality or common sense."

The defendant appealed. Affirming the lower court's judgment, the New York Court of Appeals explained:

> [The juror] and the interpreter communicated using signed English, a signing technique that transmits the speaker's words literally, without any intervening translation. The interpreter assured the court that she was familiar with and would abide by the code of ethics for sign language interpreters and that she would limit her role to that of a "communication facilitator."

The Court of Appeals also made it clear that

this appeal does not require us to determine whether a juror dependent on a nonliteral sign language, such as American Sign Language,
would be qualified under our statutory requirement that a juror be
English-speaking.

Subsequently, some other courts have cited this case as authority for
the proposition that a signing deaf juror may not be challenged for cause,
as opposed to peremptorily. When ordering the juror to serve, the court
formulated an oath for her interpreter to take based upon qualifications
expressed by the Court of Appeals in the *Guzman*. The oath requires
the interpreter to swear to interpret accurately and to take no part in
jury deliberations.

Additional Deaf Juror Experiences

Some of the other examples of deaf jury service can be found in
Randy Lee's 1989/1990 article, "Equal Protection and a Deaf Person's
Right to Serve as a Juror." Many, though not all, of the examples of
deaf jury service discussed in Lee's article came from Pennsylvania. Lee
explains that the Pennsylvania experience shows how deaf people can
gain access to jury service through lawsuits, mediation, and public education, including mock trials. Lee conducted interviews with both deaf
and hearing jurors involved in actual cases and videotaped mock trial
deliberations. Lee says that deaf jurors did not find the interpreter dis-
tracting; and after a while, the interpreter "became a court 'fixture.'"

Lee explains that in those trials involving signing interpreters in Pennsylvania, the interpreters all used Signed English because the legal system
emphasized that jurors receive not only the meaning but also the exact
words spoken. He describes Signed English as a "parallel to the English
language exactly through a combination of signs, fingerspelling, and
markers"; therefore, it "can provide the deaf juror with the necessary
exact representation of the English language spoken at trial."

Lee finds that, despite the sign-for-word structure of Signed English,
using the language presented some easily addressed concerns. First, some
hand signs may suggest more than one word. He cites as examples the
signs for BEHAVIOR and DEMEANOR, which are very similar. Potential
confusion could be resolved by mouthing the word corresponding to the
sign simultaneously.

Second, deaf people might not understand some English idioms. Citing the *DeLong* case, Lee states that an interpreter would place these idioms in context so the deaf person could understand them. He points out that this is also a problem with hearing jurors.

Third, language differences may exist between the interpreter and the potential deaf juror. "Just as in spoken English where the meanings of words may vary from community to community," he says, "the signs for words may vary slightly from one deaf community to the next." In the Pennsylvania cases, Lee did not find that to be a problem because "the jurors were all served by interpreters whom they had worked with previously and with whom they were comfortable." In situations where this is not possible, Lee suggests that before agreeing to work together, the interpreter and the potential juror communicate with one another and determine language skills, levels, and backgrounds. He said if the two could not communicate at an appropriate level, the interpreter is bound by the Code of Ethics established by the Registry of Interpreters for the Deaf to refuse the assignment. In conclusion, Lee states that Pennsylvania's experience reinforces the *Guzman* court's claim that deaf people were "as capable as anyone else of understanding technical jargon."

Lee also asserts that based on expert testimony in *DeLong,* forms of Signed English could give a deaf person an accurate representation of the English spoken at trial; therefore, the use of Signed English should not be a reason to exclude a deaf juror. The expert, in fact, testified that Ms. DeLong's exclusion "could not be justified on the basis of her impairment."

DISCUSSION

Before we address the *Guzman* court's restrictive language policy, it is important to note that the court made at least two important points. First, *Guzman* held that a deaf person could not be excluded from jury duty because of a disability. Second, the court rejected the defendant's argument that the juror was unable to understand the English language because he communicated with the court through an interpreter. The court stated that the use of an interpreter by the juror should not disqualify him as a juror.

Guzman, however, made other points, which may be considered misconceptions about sign language, interpreting, and court interpretation. The New York and Pennsylvania courts interpreted the English language requirement to allow a deaf person who communicated through Signed English to serve as a juror. On the basis of the English language requirement, both courts instructed the court-appointed interpreter to use Signed English. For the following reasons, the language policy to use only Signed English for court interpretation is inaccurate and unnecessary.

The underlying purpose of the English language requirement for jurors remains unclear. At least two possible purposes exist. One might be to exclude foreign-speaking individuals because they lack the necessary understanding of the community and its values and standards to adequately serve on a jury. If that is the case, then there are significant differences between a citizen who is deaf and a citizen who is foreign-speaking. Deaf citizens are much more likely to know the community and its values and standards. They work and participate in the community in a way that foreign-speaking persons, who are unable to speak or comprehend English, cannot.

The second possible purpose may be to exclude anyone, foreign or deaf, who requires the services of an interpreter, because of concerns about having a thirteenth person in the jury room, adequately analyzing evidence, or the possible disruption of the orderly operation of the court. The *Guzman* court dismissed all of these concerns.

Guzman was correct about the role of the interpreter, stating that he or she is not a participant, but only a communications facilitator. *Guzman* suggested that instructions to the interpreter and the jury would sufficiently address the problems of improper influence. The interpreter should be instructed that his or her only function in the jury room is to interpret and not to counsel, advise, or interject personal opinions or personally participate in any way.

The court, however, interpreted the English language requirement as disallowing the use of interpreting. The court defined a court-appointed interpreter using Signed English as a signer or transmitter, as opposed to an interpreter, explaining that when the interpreter communicated through Signed English, he or she was not interpreting, but merely transmitting the exact words in spoken English to Signed English. The court does state that Signed English is not a separate language; rather, it is English in a different form.

Another misconception that the *Guzman* court relayed is that an interpreter is a signer when that person is simply transmitting exact words in spoken English into Signed English. The process of transmitting is what we call transliterating—which converts a message in one form of a language to another form of the same language. Contrary to the court's findings, the interpreter functions as an interpreter, or at least as a transliterator.

Another point to be clarified in *Guzman* is the term Signed English. We believe that the sign system used in *Guzman* was called Pidgin Signed English, which combines a hybrid of ASL with certain forms of manually Signed English and the mouthing of English words at the same time. Since that decision, studies have found that Pidgin Signed English is a misnomer, and the appropriate term is contact signing. As explained before, contact signing varies in form, from ASL to manually coded English.

What concerns us the most about *Guzman* is that interpreters, or transliterators, should not be restricted to use only Signed English for court interpretation. Such a word-for-word or verbatim requirement is inconsistent with the standard of legal equivalence. It should be noted that *Guzman* permitted the interpreter to "express the speaker's intonation, inflection, syntax and other variations of speech through a combination of facial expressions and movements." We believe that as long as procedural safeguards to ensure the competence of interpreters are in place, courts should encourage them to interpret in such a way as to provide equivalent and accurate interpretations, rather than attempt literal interpretations of spoken discourse during the court proceedings. The issue for court interpreting, therefore, is not how to transmit a message in spoken English into contact signing, but rather to render interpretations that meet the standard of legal equivalence. This means that interpreters should be required to exploit whatever linguistic resources (including spoken English, ASL, and contact signing) are available to them to render equivalent interpretations.

RECOMMENDATIONS

Discussing how courts should clarify the role and responsibilities of court interpreters, Fallahay cited two sample oaths. One oath was taken from a 1990 New York county court case in *New York v. Green*, which appeared consistent with *Guzman.* That oath required an interpreter to swear that he or she

> will accurately *translate* from the English language into the sign language understood by the juror, who is deaf, and from that language as used by the juror into the English language . . . (Emphasis added.)

As discussed earlier, translation is linguistically impossible. The second oath that Fallahay recommended was offered by the Administrative Office of the Courts in New Jersey in 1996. This New Jersey oath requires a court-appointed interpreter to swear to "interpret accurately and impartially." The New Jersey Administrative Office also adds the following language that defines the role and responsibilities of a court interpreter:

> We are going to have an interpreter help us through these proceedings and you should know what [he/she] can do and what [he/she] cannot do. Basically, the interpreter is only here to help us communicate with each other in the proceedings. [He/she] is not a party in this case, has no interest in this case, and will be completely neutral. Accordingly, [he/she] is not working for either [party A] or [party B]. The interpreter's sole responsibility is to enable us to communicate with each other.

As Fallahay puts it, the second oath along with the clarification of the role of the interpreter is "an encapsulation of . . . the cornerstones of a qualified interpreter: effectiveness, accuracy, and impartiality."

CONCLUSION

The participation of deaf people on juries, which represents real success in the American judicial system (i.e., maintaining the right to trial by a jury of one's peers), will grow more pervasive. The court interpreter continues to play a unique role in promoting this equal right. The more this occurs, the greater the need for the courts to articulate appropriate language policies for sign language interpretation of court proceedings. The policies should incorporate accuracy as the standard by encouraging a qualified interpreter to interpret accurately.

In developing, implementing, or reviewing these language policies, the courts may want to consider the remarks of Helge Niska, whom Mikkelson quotes in her paper. To actively manage the communication process, Niska said, court interpreters should be "emancipated." She concludes:

> Being a neutral interpreter does not exclude having a sense of responsibility for the people one works with. Well-educated professional court interpreters possess good linguistic knowledge in their working languages, good interpreting technique, adequate communication skills, strong professional ethics, and have considerable knowledge about legal systems, laws, and legal procedures in the societies concerned. They also have knowledge of the various discourse situations and the language use of the various actors in the court.

> When hiring interpreters, legal professionals should opt only for the best. The interpreters should be allowed to work as professionals in their own right, as experts on human interaction and intercultural communication. This means that the interpreter must have the right to work in an optimal way to fulfill his/her task—in other words, to be obtrusive and interrupt proceedings when needed. There are bound to be conflicts . . . But in the long run, the emancipation of the interpreter will be favourable to the entire legal system and to the individuals who need language support. (1995)

REFERENCES

Administrative Office of the United States Courts. 1990. General management and administration guide to judiciary policies and procedures. In *Federal court interpreters manual: Policies and procedures*. Washington, D.C.: Author.

Administrative Office of the United States Courts. 1995. General management and administration guide to judiciary policies and procedures. In *Administrative manual*. Washington, D.C.: Author.

Court Interpreting, Legal Translating, and Bilingual Services Section, Administrative Office of the Courts of New Jersey. 1996. Standards for court interpreting, legal translating, and bilingual services. A working draft of a document prepared for the court system of New Jersey, May 22.

Fallahay, J. 2000. *The right to a full hearing. Improving access to the courts for people who are deaf or hard of hearing*. Chicago: American Judicature Society.

Frishberg, N. 1990. *Interpreting: An introduction*. Silver Spring, Md.: RID Publications.

González, R. R., V. C. Vasquez, and H. Mikkelson. 1991. *Court interpretation: Theory, policy and practice.* Durham, N.C.: Carolina Academic Press.

Hewitt, W. E. 1995. *Court interpretation: Model guides for policy and practice in the state courts.* Williamsburg, Va.: National Center for State Courts.

Lee, R. 1989/1990. Equal protection and a deaf person's right to serve as a juror. *New York University Review of Law and Social Change* 17:81–117.

Lucas, C., and C. Valli. 1992. *Language contact in the American Deaf community.* New York: Academic Press.

Mikkelson, H. 2000a. Verbatim interpretation: An oxymoron. Available [on-line]: http://www.acebo.com/papers/verbatim.htm.

———. 2000b. Towards a redefinition of the role of the court interpreter. Available [on-line]: http://www.acebo.com/papers/rolintrp.htm.

Morris, R. 1995. Pragmatism, precept and passions: The attitudes of English-language legal systems to non-English speakers. In *Translation and the law*, ed. M. Morris. American Translators Association Scholarly Monograph Series, vol. 8. Amsterdam and Philadelphia: John Benjamins.

Niska, H. 1995. Just interpreting: Role conflicts and discourse types in court interpreting. In *Translation and the law*, ed. M. Morris. American Translators Association Scholarly Monograph Series, vol. 8. Amsterdam and Philadelphia: John Benjamins.

U.S. Department of Justice. 1993. *Title II technical assistance manual covering state and local government programs and services.* Washington, D.C.: Government Printing Office. Available [on-line]: http://www.usdoj.gov/crt/ada/taman2.html.

———. 1997a. Settlement agreement between the United States of America and Harrison County, Mississippi (DJ #204–41-2) (1997). Available [on-line]: http://www.usdoj.gov/crt/ada/harriss.htm.

———. 1997b. Settlement agreement under the Americans with Disabilities Act of 1990 between the United States of America and Philadelphia Court of Common Pleas, Pennsylvania (DJ #204–62-106). Available [on-line]: http://www.usdoj.gov/crt/ada/settlemt.htm#anchor502508.

———. 2002. Nondiscrimination on the basis of disability in state and local government services, 35 C.F.R. part 35. Available [on-line]: http://www.usdoj.gov/crt/ada/reg2.html.

When "Equal" Means "Unequal"—

And Other Legal Conundrums

for the Deaf Community

Sarah S. Geer

Laws structure our society and interactions; they affect all of us, every day, in large and in small ways. Laws are made of words. Therefore, the use and interpretation of legal language is unusually important. Understanding legal language is important to lawyers and judges, of course, but also to the rest of society, as our decisions and lives are controlled by laws and judicial actions.

Lawyers and judges use words as their primary tools. Lawyers spend most of their workdays immersed in language: reading, speaking, listening, and writing. It is commonly said that one of the primary tasks of law school is to indoctrinate new students into talking and writing "like a lawyer." Unfortunately, talking like a lawyer is not always a complimentary term! Legal language is characterized by formality, complexity, verbosity, and the use of arcane terminology.

The result is obvious: Nonlawyers frequently misunderstand lawyers, legal terms, and laws. Most Americans would correctly define an *assault* as a violent physical attack. For example, one might say, "He was assaulted in a dark alley." This is how the term is defined in English dictionaries. To a lawyer, however, an assault, as defined under common law principles, involves no physical contact at all. It is merely a threat to make physical contact. To a lawyer, the assault victim in that dark alley may have been scared and may have been threatened, and he may even have fallen down backwards over a garbage can and been physically injured, but he was not physically touched in any way by the person who assaulted him. If a fist, finger, or foot actually makes physical contact with another person, a lawyer calls that act a *battery*.

Words such as *equal, disability, reasonable, appropriate, effective,* and *rights* have highly specific legal meanings in the context of courts and lawsuits. Some of those meanings come as a surprise to nonlawyers. The meanings of these words may seem especially counterintuitive to members of the Deaf community who receive both the vernacular meaning and the legal meaning through yet a third language, American Sign Language (ASL), or other sign language variants.

Legal jargon is more than a static professional vocabulary. It has power. Judges and legislatures take words from the ordinary vernacular and ascribe definitions literally "as a matter of law," which may be different from the meaning of these words in everyday discourse. This language planning takes place in three forums, as laws are written by legislatures, implemented by executive agencies, and interpreted in courts.

Like language itself, legal terms can change substantially over time both in terms of policy and meaning. In *FCC v. Pottsville Broadcasting Co.,* the U.S. Supreme Court described a legal term, the *public interest* standard in the Federal Communications Act, as a "supple instrument" for the agency to use to carry out the legislative policy that was broadly established by Congress.[1] The suppleness of law can be both a strength and a weakness. Congress has granted similar authority to the U.S. Department of Justice (DOJ), the U.S. Department of Education, and other executive agencies to create, interpret, and implement the disability rights laws of the past twenty-five years.[2] Over time, our understanding of some of the terms used in these laws has changed.

This paper will examine some of the interpretations that have been imposed on selected key terms in the landmark federal laws that most directly affect deaf and hard of hearing people in the United States. These laws include the Americans with Disabilities Act (ADA), Section 504 of the Rehabilitation Act of 1973, and the Individuals with Disabilities Education Act.[3] Relevant legal language is found in the statutory terms enacted by Congress and in the associated regulatory language developed by federal executive agencies. Finally, these terms have been used and defined in court cases, in which judges take those statutory and regulatory terms and apply them to specific factual controversies in written decisions. Some illustrative cases will be examined in each section. This paper is not a comprehensive explanation of the laws, which is far beyond its scope.

Key terms will also be briefly examined in the context of how they are understood by members of the general public and by the Deaf and hard of hearing community. Other papers in this volume analyze in depth the challenges inherent in the interpretation of legal terms into sign language. For example, the concept of a legal right to remain silent can be elusive to an ASL user, depending on whether the term *right* is rendered as a legal right (strong, mandatory term), as *alright* (a weak, permissive term), or as *correct* (an inappropriate term in this context). Each of these meanings has great significance for the behavior of a deaf person accused of a crime. Depending on how the suspect reacts to the *Miranda* warnings, his or her defense to a criminal charge may be either compromised or strengthened.

Similar confusions arise when looking at typical language that appears in the most important nondiscrimination laws that affect people with disabilities. As a result, members of the Deaf community sometimes experience frustration and confusion in understanding how the civil rights laws affect them. A simple example is in the title of the Americans with Disabilities Act; despite its name, the law applies to all persons who are deaf or hard of hearing in the United States, regardless of whether they are American citizens. Deaf citizens of other countries have the same rights under the ADA as American citizens while they are in this country. However, the ADA usually does not apply to deaf or hard of hearing American citizens when they are traveling or living in other countries. American laws are only effective within the territorial borders of the United States.[4]

Defining the meanings of words and terms is a frequent task of judges and legislators. Some do this analysis well; some do it badly. Disability law is in constant flux as a result of confusion about some critical terms, such as the definition of a person with a disability or understanding a reasonable accommodation for a deaf employee.

CHARACTERISTIC FEATURES AND JUSTIFICATIONS
FOR LEGAL LANGUAGE: THE GOOD, THE BAD, AND THE UGLY

Before looking at some specific terms as they appear in our statutes and jurisprudence, it is helpful to examine typical features of legal language and the forums in which it is written. Criticism of legal language is virtually a cottage industry; indictments of legalese and its users are common. However, some of the peculiarities of legal language have important purposes.

Obscurity

Legalese and legal writing are easily identifiable from other types of discourse. Legal documents often involve pompous, convoluted, and dense sentences; repetition and negation; passive voice; and archaic terminology. A legal restatement of a familiar classic goes as follows:

The party of the first part hereinafter known as Jack . . . and the party of the second part hereinafter known as Jill . . . ascended or caused to be ascended an elevation of undetermined height and degree of slope, hereinafter referred to as "hill." Whose purpose it was to obtain, attain, procure, secure or otherwise gain acquisition to, by any and/or all means available to them a receptacle or container, hereinafter known as "pail," suitable for the transport of a liquid whose chemical properties shall be limited to hydrogen and oxygen, the proportions of which shall not be less than or exceed two parts for the first mentioned element and one part for the latter. Such combination will hereinafter be called "water." On the occasion stated above, it has been established beyond reasonable doubt that Jack did plunge, tumble, topple, or otherwise be caused to lose his footing in a manner that caused his body to be thrust into a downward direction. As a direct result of these combined circumstances, Jack suffered fractures and contusions of the bones of his cranial regions. Jill, whether due to Jack's misfortune or not, was known to also tumble in similar fashion after Jack. (Whether the term "after" shall be interpreted in a spatial or time passage sense has not been determined.)[5]

In spite of its opaque style, legal language is essential to our lives. It appears in our everyday discussions of marriage and divorce, car accidents, speeding tickets, landlords, and credit cards. We sign three-page leases and seven-page contracts and loan documents to buy cars without blinking at the lines and lines of legalese in tiny fonts. Legal notices appear in every workplace. In theory, these notices are intended to inform employees about their rights to a safe workplace or their rights to be free from discrimination. In practice, few employees can decipher the terms of the standard OSHA (Occupational Safety and Health Administration) notices.

Disability discrimination laws also require the posting of legal notices. The ADA and Section 504 of the Rehabilitation Act require employers and places of public accommodation to give "notice" that they do not discriminate on the basis of disability. In other words, signs must be posted to inform the public that the institution does not discriminate on the basis of disability. A typical lawyer-drafted notice for Section 504 might read:

> No otherwise qualified person with a disability shall be excluded from the participation in, be denied the benefits of, or be subjected to discrimination under any program or activity conducted by this recipient of federal financial assistance.

A lawyer-drafted notice that is very important to a deaf person might read:

> This place of public accommodation shall furnish appropriate auxiliary aids and services where necessary to ensure effective communication with individuals with disabilities.

How many people, deaf or hearing, would understand this sign to mean that interpreters are available for deaf people on request, at no charge? Technically, these notices comply with the law. Adherence to the *formal* language of the law is deemed legally sufficient, even though nothing is functionally communicated.

Language must be judged in terms of the social purposes it serves. The obscure phrases in these notices actually serve important, desirable functions for the lawyer who drafted the notice and for the business that posted it. First, the lawyer can be confident that the notice does technically comply with the law, since it includes the precise words used in the statute. Therefore, the lawyer's client runs no risk of liability. Second, the business can be confident that it will not get many requests for expensive services such as interpreters, since the vast majority of the reading public will have no idea that the notice means that interpreters are available.

The National Association of the Deaf (NAD) Law Center has argued successfully that this type of legal notice is meaningless if the people who need the information do not get it. Instead, the NAD advocates the use of plain English notices about policies and services that comply with the law. After a lawsuit brought by the NAD Law Center, a hospital posted the following signs:

> Maine Medical Center provides sign language interpreting services, telecommunication devices (TTYs), and other aids and services to

persons who are deaf or hard of hearing. These services are provided by MMC free of charge. Please ask for assistance at Room [22].[6]

The notice could be simplified and clarified even further. It could also be made broader by listing services for people with other disabilities, such as

Free Equipment and Services for People with Disabilities Available in Room 22:

- sign language interpreters
- TTYs
- Braille materials
- Other equipment and services for people with disabilities

Reworking the notice to be understandable would better serve the readers of the sign, but it might be less satisfactory to the lawyer and the business. The value of legal language must be judged by the purposes that are served in the writing. In the case of the ADA and Section 504, law establishes the purpose of the notice: to inform people with disabilities about services and accommodations.

Self-Identification and Economic Self-Interest

Why would the legal profession countenance the use of peculiar, impenetrable language? One function is a lawyer's apparent need for self-identification and self-aggrandizement. Sociologists understand that every profession uses rituals, symbols, and codes to set it apart from the rest of the world. Using legal language signifies immediately that a person is in fact a lawyer, a member of the club, with any social status that might be associated with this profession.[7] In spite of widespread public antipathy toward lawyers, a law degree does connote professional status on the basis of a relatively high level of education and sophistication.

Other observers have noted that typical legal language provides a lawyer with professional protection. There is an economic rationale for prolix legal writing: It creates a clientele. If contracts, wills, complaints, and deeds can only be understood by lawyers, then the public will need to hire legal services on a regular basis to write or interpret the meaning of these crucial documents.

Consumer protection advocates have successfully pressed for laws that require legal documents and statutes to be written in plain English.[8]

Some state laws require consumer contracts and insurance policies to be written in plain English. New York uses a subjective plain language standard: A covered agreement must be written in a "clear and coherent manner" using words with "common and everyday meanings."[9] Other statutes use objective standards. For example, the Model Life and Health Insurance Policy Language Simplification Act, enacted in many jurisdictions, requires insurance policies in these states to achieve a minimum score of 40 on the Flesch Reading Ease Test, which takes into account sentence length and the number of syllables per word.[10] President Carter issued an executive order in 1978, requiring government regulations to be written in plain English.[11] More recently, the Securities and Exchange Commission has required stock prospectuses to be written in plain language.[12] These efforts toward plain English are slowly being introduced into the writing programs at law schools, but the pace of change is very slow.

Archaic Terminology and Ritualistic Language

Legal language is linguistically conservative. It contains much old formality that has long outlived its usefulness. The first line of a deed or contract may recite the phrase "Know all men by these presents." The last line of an affidavit is often the phrase "And further affiant sayeth not." A plaintiff in an ADA complaint may ask a court for specific remedies (including an award of money) and then ask "for such other and further relief as to the Court may seem meet and just." Other typical legal words are remnants of Old and Middle English that could easily be omitted or replaced by modern English, including *whereas, to wit, hereby, hereinafter, herewith, aforesaid, therein, forthwith*, and *witnesseth*.[13] Yet lawyers cling tenaciously to the old forms. The resulting use of anachronistic language can sound very strange to the contemporary ear.

This extreme conservatism is due, at least in part, to the reverence of our judicial systems for written codes. One effect of writing is to freeze or preserve that language over time. Some of the earliest human writings were efforts to write down the words that make up laws. Among the best known early efforts to collect social laws and customs into formal codes are the Code of Hammurabi, circa 1700 B.C.E., the writings that comprise the Mosaic Code (Law of Moses), circa 1000–400 B.C.E., the Athenian code of Solon, circa 590 B.C.E., and Justinian's *Corpus Juris*

Civilis (Body of Civil Law), circa 533. Through history, written codes of laws have become increasingly complex and detailed.

The availability of a formal written code means that the words and phrases of the past are still living legal concepts. Under our system of applied law, lawyers and judges revere written codes as authoritative textual authority for the legal principles they are applying. As courts have used legal language and issued legal decisions over time, they have formally defined and refined the meanings of those terms. Terms in the oldest legal texts are still used, and their meanings are clearly understood by the trained legal professional.

Therefore, it is not surprising that our current jurisprudence retains the language of the 1700s, as written in the Constitution, the first U.S. Code, and the first rules of procedures used in federal courts. These codes, of course, borrowed heavily from much earlier English and French legal codes. Thomas Jefferson, when revising the laws of Virginia after the Declaration of Independence, was eager to simplify the verbose English codes, while "preserving the very words of the established law, wherever their meaning had been sanctioned by judicial decisions or rendered technical by usage."[14] Despite many amendments, much of the original language remains in the U.S. Code and the Federal Rules of Civil Procedure today, as copied from ancient English statutes.

This tendency to retain outdated language is evident even in the recent disability statutes. The original language of Section 504 of the Rehabilitation Act referred to "handicapped persons." The statute has been amended and now uses the term *persons with disabilities*. This new term emphasizes the person rather than the person's physical status and uses *disability* rather than *handicap* to refer to that status. Many people requested this change because they found the old terminology offensive, and the amendment of Section 504 became part of the ADA. However, the all-important regulations that implement the law have never been amended, probably due to administrative inertia. The regulations still use the term *handicapped person*.[15] Some clients are outraged to see themselves referred to in legal briefs as handicapped persons, a name they consider demeaning and obsolete. However, a lawyer attempting to rely on the regulation, only fifteen years old, must fit his or her argument into the formal written text. People who are deaf and do not consider themselves to be either handicapped or disabled must accept the terms of the ADA and Section 504 if they wish to avail themselves of the laws' protections against discrimination.

The words of former judges are equally as potent as the words of legislators. Our legal system is built on the doctrine of *stare decisis* (the thing has already been decided). In this system, precedent controls. A previous ruling on similar facts virtually mandates a similar holding in the future. Because of this reverence for precedent, phrases and holdings of early judicial opinions are constantly cited and alluded to in contemporary legal arguments. Almost any formal legal writing (including this paper) will be proudly decorated with notes citing phrases from previous cases and legal sources to buttress the credibility of the writer's arguments. Legal periodicals are notorious for pages that consist of a few lines of text at the top of the page, with the majority of the page devoted to closely spaced, densely written footnotes full of citation numbers.

Terms of Art

Some arcane phrases and terms are retained for solid professional reasons. If a term is defined in a statute or if a court has defined a term, a lawyer in that jurisdiction can feel comfortable in using and applying it. All lawyers will know what it means. The average reader has no idea what the phrase *nunc pro tunc* (now for then) might mean, but a lawyer will instantly recognize the term for something that is given retroactive effect (i.e., backdated).[16]

Recycling well-used language is also extremely convenient and economical, even if it no longer fits contemporary rhetoric. Formbooks are developed for lawyers that reprint standard or model contract language, complaints, wills, or jury instructions, along with the authority for using that particular form. Lawyers were among the first to take up computer word processing, since it enables them to insert appropriate names and facts easily into the standard forms and templates of legal documents.

These formbooks and templates do not always give us the clearest legal writing.[17] They use phrases and provisions that are familiar and do not require a lawyer to develop language from scratch. This saves a lawyer significant time and effort and minimizes the risk of making errors by acting independently.[18] Formbooks are responsible for the continued use of hoary phrases such as "party of the first part" in standard contracts. Although Agostino's ADA formbook contains many examples of clear legal drafting, it includes the classic legal phrases and circumlocutions that read so strangely.[19] For example, the employment discrimination models generally contain an assertion that the complaint was "timely filed" by the plaintiff with the Equal Employment Opportunity Commission (EEOC). This obsolete phrase will continue to live on in the formbooks, even though "filed on time" is standard English for what the lawyer is saying.

The models also invariably contain an allegation that "the EEOC has issued plaintiff a right to sue letter." The grammar of this sentence presents many peculiarities. It is certainly confusing to anyone who does not know that when employees file a complaint of discrimination with the EEOC, it eventually writes ("issues") each employee a letter advising them of their right to sue their employer in a court. Lawyers and courts familiar with the EEOC procedure abbreviate this into the phrase "right to sue letter." A lawyer uses these phrases so routinely that it may take conscious effort to re-cast them into plain English.

Similar baffling shorthand is used to describe established constitutional principles of equal rights. In briefs, opinions, and arguments, lawyers and judges debate whether people with disabilities should be considered to belong to a "suspect class" or a "quasi-suspect class." To most people, being called part of a suspect class would undoubtedly have a negative connotation. A suspect is ordinarily thought of as one who is believed to be guilty of something, sometimes on little or no evidence. Something that is suspect is considered bad, harmful, or questionable. A suspect thing or person is viewed with distrust and suspicion.

Amazingly, however, a suspect class in constitutional rhetoric refers to a specially favored group that is entitled to the highest degree of protection under the Equal Protection Clause of the Constitution.[20] African Americans are a suspect class, entitled to protected status under constitutional law. Here is the source of the rhetorical confusion: Lawyers are using the term *suspect class* as a crude shorthand for the term *suspect classification*. The word *suspect* does not describe the group that needs protection. Instead, it refers to the state law that classifies or singles out the protected group. If a law denies the vote to people of African American heritage, the court will consider that law suspect and will examine it closely to see if there is any way to justify the law under the Constitution.[21] What is suspect is not the person, but the act of the legislature, which adopted a statute that has created a classification or distinction on the basis of race or religion. However, because these cases all refer liberally to "classes" of persons, the phrase *suspect class* has become the shorthand for the principle itself. Lawyers understand and accept this usage, although it makes no sense from a grammatical or logical perspective.

Phrases like *a right to sue letter* or *suspect class* are convenient shorthand for lawyers and judges. Similarly, complex concepts of law are truncated into the name of the case in which the legal proposition was first clarified. Therefore, lawyers can confidently refer to a *Miranda* warning or an *Allen* charge, knowing that they will be understood by lawyers and judges.

Scholars and linguists may refer to these terms as jargon (specialized vocabulary of a trade, occupation, or profession). Lawyers prefer the more flattering *term of art* to describe their specialized vocabulary.[22] Examples of useful terms of art with precise legal meanings include *chilling effect, grandfather clause, sidebar,* or *judge-shopping.* Tiersma characterizes jargon as objectionable when it is useless and can be easily replaced with standard English. For example, lawyers frequently use *indicate* to mean *say* (e.g., I indicated to the judge . . .) or *implicate* for *relates to* or *invokes* (e.g., Plaintiff's argument implicates the First Amendment.).[23] Examples of legal jargon that are probably not terms of art include typical lawyer-like phrases such as *arguendo, case at bar, case on point, case on all fours, conclusory,* and *instant case.*

An example of a technical term of art is *dictum,* referring to language in a judge's decision that is not directly relevant to the legal issues being decided. Lawyers analyzing cases for meaningful precedent can safely ignore "mere dictum" in a judge's opinion. In *Rothschild v. Grottenthaler,* deaf parents sued under Section 504 when a public school refused to provide interpreters when the parents met with their hearing child's teacher.[24] The U.S. Court of Appeals for the Second Circuit ruled that a school district must provide a sign language interpreter for deaf parents who are attending meetings with teachers about a child's academics or disciplinary issues. The court decision also included some discussion of the child's eventual graduation ceremony, suggesting that the school district would not be required to provide an interpreter for that purpose since the ceremony was not part of the curriculum and the parents would be attending voluntarily. Graduation ceremonies, school plays, and other noncurricular events were not a part of the original lawsuit. Lawyers for deaf parents would be quick to dismiss this part of the opinion as "mere dictum." Lawyers for school districts would disagree and claim that the discussion of graduation ceremonies is not dictum; it is an inseparable part of the ruling. Although the lawyers may argue about the scope of the holding, both groups would agree on the definition of the term itself.

Need for Precision

Laws should be clear and precise, because it would be unfair to subject a person to repercussions for breaking a rule that is not clearly understood. It is desirable to have rules of law that are clearly understood, so that people can conform their conduct to them and anticipate the results of legal decision making.

Many of the unusual features of legal writing come from an effort to be precise. David Mellinkoff is rueful about the precision of legal language, but he understands why it is necessary to make it so.[25] One of his "Rules of Legal Writing" states:

> Some day someone will read what you have written, trying to find something wrong with it. This is the special burden of legal writing, and the special incentive to be as precise as you can.[26]

For example, legal phrases are often comically redundant. Typical usages are *null and void; fit and proper; rest, residue, and remainder; due and payable, over, above, and in addition to;* and *force and effect.* This verbosity originates from a professional effort to be as comprehensive and precise as possible, listing every alternative that may remotely apply. A will is titled "Last Will and Testament" on the basis of a fifteenth century belief that a *will* (from Old English) was the appropriate document to dispose of land and a *testament* (from Latin) was the appropriate document for gifts of personal property (chattels).[27] Contemporary law no longer recognizes this distinction, and the word *last* is unnecessary, so the document could be simply titled "Will." It seldom is.

In a will, it is common for the testator to "give, devise, and bequeath" property. This apparent redundancy also derives from understandable legal caution, given the background of these words. They are not historically synonyms. Under common law principles and by legal custom, the word *devise* (from Old French) has a very specific meaning. It applies only to *real* property (i.e., realty and land). The word *bequeath* (from Old English) is equally specific. It originally applied only to personal property and specific gifts of money. Therefore, if someone writing a will simply "bequeaths" her property to her brother, the brother might only be able to claim her car, household furnishings, and other personal property, unless he can prove that his sister intended to leave him her house and money as well. To protect beneficiaries (and themselves), lawyers are accustomed to include all of the words that connote gifts, so that the beneficiary will be certain to get everything the testator intended. Contemporary legal scholars scorn this usage and recommend using only the word *give*, which is clear in meaning and comprehensive in intent.[28] *Give* is just as precise as *give, devise, and bequeath* and subject to less possibility of error.

Need for Vagueness

In other contexts, however, legal practitioners intentionally choose words and phrases that are imprecise and vague. The most obvious example of this is the legal standard for negligence, which is defined within the context of what a "reasonable man" would or would not do. Goldstein and Lieberman assert that the legal requirement that a person act "reasonably" is impossible to define. They consider this a virtue, since there are too many variables in human conduct to account for in the concept of negligence.[29] Although the reasonable man standard persists, it has little practical meaning. Negligence cases are inevitably decided on a case-by-case basis.

Writing with vagueness can be sound policy, since legal concepts must often be sufficiently encompassing to fit changing circumstances. Certain legal concepts benefit from being inherently vague, such as *due process, equal protection of the laws,* or *executive power.* [30] For example, traditional jurisprudence requires judges to make custody decisions "in the best interests of the child." This so-called rule of law gives judges the widest possible latitude, under the guise of a formal legal standard. It is really not a rule at all, since no one can apply this standard to foresee how a judge might actually decide a custody case. Developing an easily measured rule for child custody would not be difficult. Such a rule might give custody of a child to the child's mother, or to the parent with the most assets, or to the parent who can give a child a two-parent home. Such rules would be easy to apply, and parents would be certain how a custody argument would be decided. But this would not necessarily be in the "best interests" of the child. Often, intangible or unusual features must be considered in placing children. For example, if a child is deaf and uses sign language, custody decisions should be strongly influenced by whether a parent has competency in sign language and can communicate effectively with the child.

Justice Benjamin Cardozo wrote extensively about the craft of judging and the problems of writing legal decisions. He was particularly interested in the tension between the need for the law to be both sufficiently malleable to accommodate new cases as they arise and sufficiently rigid to define rights and responsibilities reliably.[31]

> No doubt the ideal system, if it were attainable, would be a code at once so flexible and so minute, as to supply in advance for every conceivable situation the just and fitting rule. But life is too complex to bring the attainment of this ideal within the compass of human powers.[32]

Vague and elastic terms in legal decisions or statutes allow the law to change and grow with changing circumstances and technology. The Fourth Amendment prohibition against "unreasonable searches and seizures" was written before electricity had any practical application. The same words can be applied today to a world that includes electronic eavesdropping, computer hacking, and powerful surveillance devices. The standard (unreasonable searches and seizures) is vague enough to encompass current technology unknown at the time the phrase was uttered.

The telecommunications arena is a perfect example of the problems created when over-precise language cannot grow with changing technology. The original Communications Act of 1934 applied only to "wire and radio service" and is codified under a chapter titled "Telegraphs, Telephones and Radiotelegraphs."[33] It is still codified under the original section and title, but the statute has had to be regularly amended in ways to permit it to regulate the vast new fields of television, cable, satellite transmission, and now Web communications.

The Deaf community has had to be diligent to make sure the Communications Act keeps pace with changing technology. In 1977, deaf advocates successfully petitioned the Federal Communications Commission (FCC) to order television broadcasters to begin using captions and provide emergency information visually as well as aurally.[34] No longer would deaf viewers see a caption stating Emergency Bulletin while a useless voice-over provided critical emergency information. At that time, the captioning system was in its infancy.[35] The development of captioning since 1977 has been dramatic, and the FCC is now enforcing new standards that will require 95 percent of new broadcasts to be captioned by 2006.[36] However, these and other more recent captioning orders applied only to analog television and to captioning carried on the Line 21 transmission band. The order is precisely worded, so it does not cover the technology necessary for the anticipated development of digital television receivers. The appearance of digital television receivers required yet more FCC regulations. Alert advocates for the Deaf community anticipated this problem, petitions were filed with the FCC, and the FCC acted. Digital receivers must now have captioning capability, just as analog receivers do.[37] The battle is not over, however. New Web technologies overlap broadcast, cable, and telephone mechanisms. The television captioning requirements appear not to apply when a consumer uses a personal computer monitor instead of a television receiver to capture television content. Therefore, it appears that yet another rule making and order will be necessary to clarify the captioning requirements for this new medium. Precise standards are necessary, but as a result, four major sets of standards have been adopted in the past fifteen years, and more will be necessary.

Precision in legal drafting can have unintended consequences. Title III of the Americans with Disabilities Act applies to all "places of public accommodation." It is clear from the legislative history that this term was intended to have the broadest possible application, so that people with disabilities would be protected from discrimination in more than five million private businesses, nonprofit organizations, and professional and service establishments.[38] The definition of a place of public accommodation specifically includes the "office of an accountant or lawyer."[39] Thanks to the ADA, lawyers must routinely hire sign language interpreters when meeting with deaf clients, and lawyers must use the relay system or e-mail to communicate with deaf clients. However, some attorneys have forcefully argued that the ADA would NOT apply to meetings with clients that do not occur within their actual *place* of business (such as a hallway conference at a courthouse or a meeting at a client's home). Fortunately, the ADA has generally been interpreted to cover all the services of an office of a lawyer, which would include activities that take place off-site.

The development of the Internet and other forms of distance commerce have raised new issues in interpreting a word such as *place*. In recent years, a significant amount of commercial activity has moved to the Internet and to mail order or telephone operations. Some e-businesses may never deal with customers face to face and may operate without a physical place or location. There is an ongoing argument over whether such businesses are subject to the ADA.[40] If the ADA were being written today, it would without a doubt specifically include Internet businesses, and it would either avoid the word *place* or define it to include an Internet location or URL (uniform resource locator). The argument about the applicability of the ADA to the Internet does not affect most people with disabilities, who have no problems with Internet access; they are more concerned with physical access into places and the behavior of employees in commercial entities. It is vitally important to deaf people, however, who may find business communication easier using e-mail, TTYs, and other electronic methods, rather than in face-to-face interactions. Initially, computer communication was a great boon to deaf and blind consumers since it avoided the need to travel physically to a store or to speak with service providers. The advent of mouse technology and graphical user interfaces created new barriers for blind users, however, who could not locate the links between Web pages. In the next phase of computer development, deaf users may be closed out from Web programming that is based on voice streaming and voice recognition technology.

The tension between vagueness and precision, flexibility and rigidity, is an inevitable part of writing legal codes and decisions. The ADA approaches this dilemma with two parallel solutions. Some essential phrases are intentionally vague and open-ended, especially *reasonable accommodation* and *undue burden*. These phrases must be interpreted on a case-by-case basis by the courts in the common law tradition.[41]

On the other hand, the ADA has generated a massive amount of highly specific statutory, regulatory, and interpretive language as specific as a building code in terms of permissible doorway widths, sink heights, flooring materials, and loudness and brightness of building alarm systems. The statute itself takes up fifty-two pages in its final, printed public law form. Officials have also produced twelve sets of detailed regulations by the EEOC, the DOJ, the Department of Transportation, the Architectural and Transportation Barriers Compliance Board, and the FCC. In addition, these agencies issued massive amounts of technical assistance manuals and booklets with examples, model policies, and guidance on compliance with the ADA.

According to a senator who was involved with the ADA and watches it with interest, "The obvious hope on the part of the agencies is that volume equals clarity. On the other hand, this volume may erect barriers for small businesses whose owners or managers have limited time and resources to invest in mastering the federal regulations and advisories."[42]

The resulting body of disability law has some interesting interpretive booby traps that ensnare lawyers, judges, the disability community, and the general public.

HOW LEGAL LANGUAGE IS DEVELOPED

Legal language is directly influenced by the institutional and historical contexts in which law is made. American federal law is developed in three major forums: legislatures, executive agencies, and courts. Each forum has its own institutional pressures that affect language choices. The results are not always well-reasoned. Imagine a harried legislator, attending interminable committee meetings, voting on bills in areas in which he or she has little expertise, perhaps agreeing to modify the language in one proposed law in exchange for another legislator's support on a different bill. Think of long hallways of bureaucrats, each writing pages of minute regulations in their own obscure area of expertise. See a judge writing an opinion that is not reviewed by any supervisor or colleague, covering up a fundamental lack of knowledge of a subject by overstating the certainty of a legal principle: "There is no doubt whatsoever that under the laws of the land, . . . "

Legislative Process: Enactment of a Statute

The very first section of our Constitution, article 1 section 1, states that:

All legislative Powers herein granted shall be vested in a Congress of the United States, which shall consist of a Senate and House of Representatives.

It is a long and winding road from an idea to a law. There are numerous opportunities along the way for language to be considered and altered. Because any bill goes through several processing steps that require majority action, the bill is subject to political pressures and compromises at every step of the way.

The consideration and debate process can seem endless. The federal process begins with the introduction of a formal, written bill or sometimes as a joint resolution in the Senate or the House of Representatives.[43] The idea for a new law can come from anywhere—a member of Congress; a constituent, lobbyist, or organization who petitions for a bill to be drafted; a legislative committee; or an executive communication from the president, the president's cabinet, or a federal agency. Deaf and disability advocates such as NAD and the Disability Rights Education and Defense Fund (DREDF) have been active in proposing and supporting new legislative initiatives. However, only a legislator can formally introduce and sponsor a bill. The actual drafting process will depend on the method by which the bill was developed. Legislators have been elected through the political process; they may not be lawyers or trained in legislative drafting. Therefore, the legislator frequently turns to a special office of professional legal writers for help in translating the legislative goal into appropriate language.

Each bill may go through formal hearings and is accompanied by committee reports, including minority and dissenting views. After debate and a series of readings, the bill will be voted on, and if successful, will become an "act" of the House or Senate. The act is then referred to the other chamber of the Congress, where it must also be referred to committee and considered. A bill cannot become law unless both chambers of Congress agree on precisely the same language. The complex rules of debate and consideration of bills differ slightly in the House and the Senate, but the overall procedure is congruent.[44] Acts of Congress are then assigned a new public law number (as in P.L. 94-142, the 142nd Act passed by the 94th Congress).[45]

Every word of the process of legislative deliberation is retained as part of the legislative history of the bill—every draft of the bill, witness statements, all committee reports and supplemental views of members, and all discussion from the floor of the House or Senate. All are published as part of the formal record of the Congress.

Executive Process: Promulgation of Regulations

Enacting a statute may not be the end, but only the beginning, of lawmaking. In the post–New Deal era, delegation to administrative agencies has become the dominant means of implementation. Non-elected agency employees have enormous authority to make legal policy and set legal standards in the context of rule making (the adoption of regulations).[46]

Historically, the legislative branch was, by definition, the lawmaking branch of government. Today, debate rages among legal scholars, specifically the new "legal process" and "strict construction" schools, as to the primacy of legislative language choices over the decisions of courts or the implementation of law-like regulations by agencies. The experience of federal disability legislation is a case in point.

After a law is enacted and codified, it is often necessary for one of the executive agencies to promulgate regulations to implement the law. Laws are the product of so much political compromise that they often contain vague phrases and general principles. Section 504 of the Rehabilitation Act of 1973 is a typical example. This law, which has been a crucial part of disability law for thirty years, consists of only one sentence:

> No otherwise qualified individual with a disability in the United States, as defined in section 706(8) . . . shall, solely by reason of her or his disability, be excluded from the participation in, be denied the benefits of, or subjected to discrimination under any program or activity receiving Federal financial assistance or under any program or activity conducted by any Executive agency or by the United States Postal Service.[47]

The heart of this law is clear: No person with a disability shall be subjected to discrimination under federally funded programs or federal programs. But there are no specifics. What disabilities are protected? What does a federal program have to do to prevent discrimination? Must they build ramps? How steep? Must they hire interpreters for deaf people or use written notes? Should they buy braille books for blind readers? Should they install TTYs? If so, how many? Does a program have to hire a certain number of people with disabilities? If so, how many? And how does a person who has experienced discrimination from a federal program get any justice? To whom do they complain?

Congress could not decide these details. The process would be both highly inefficient and politically volatile. Laws could never be passed if the members of Congress had to reach consensus on all of these issues. Instead, Congress may authorize federal agencies to write regulations to spell out the implementation of the general principle they have enacted. Although the regulations are not laws, they are enforced like laws in the courts. Regulations can be struck down if they go beyond the statute that authorizes them; but generally, courts will defer to the expertise of agency rule makers. Courts give deference to the resulting regulations as if they were law.

It would appear to be a sensible method of lawmaking. Congress sets general policy, and more precise regulations are written with the benefit of the expertise of professional agency staff, with policy direction from the President and political appointees at the head of each agency. Proposed rules are always published in the *Federal Register* and given a period for public comment. Hearings may also be held. Eventually, the regulations are formally issued and printed in the *Code of Federal Regulations*, which has a numbering system similar to that of the U.S. Code.

In the case of Section 504, this was a tumultuous process. The statute itself does not explicitly order any specific agency to adopt regulations. Section 504 was a "stealth amendment" to the Vocational Rehabilitation Act of 1974, which provided funding for many employment and social service rehabilitation programs. Civil rights language was quietly inserted in Title V of the act, apparently to ensure that people who received disability rehabilitation would not be foreclosed from job opportunities due to discrimination.[48] President Gerald Ford assigned the U.S. Department of Health, Education and Welfare (HEW) (later divided into the U.S. Department of Education and the U.S. Department of Health and Human Services [HHS]) as the lead agency to draft the original Section 504 regulation. Years went by as HEW officials held public hearings and considered the issues of disability discrimination, but they failed to issue a regulation. Finally, after increasingly angry public protests, several formal petitions, wheelchair/disability sit-ins, and a lawsuit, HEW issued its regulations on January 13, 1978.[49,50]

It is not a coincidence that the language of Section 504 reads similarly to the Civil Rights Act of 1964. John Wodatch and his staff at HEW's Office for Civil Rights (OCR) wrote the Section 504 regulations on the basis of OCR's history of dealing with discrimination on the basis of race and segregation.[51] As a result, the Section 504 regulations are expressed as affirmative legal mandates. If the regulations had been assigned to a traditional service agency, such as the Rehabilitation Services Administration, it is possible that they would have been stated very differently, perhaps in the context of community education programs and requests for voluntary compliance among recipients of federal assistance.[52] Instead, the regulations established standards for physical accessibility, and demanded "equal" access to public services and facilities. The regulations require publicly assisted schools to admit students with disabilities and to provide auxiliary services necessary for these students to benefit from the curriculum. Similar mandates were written for social service and health care agencies.

The National Council on Disability asserts that the language of the Section 504 regulations helped change the way people think about people with disabilities. As one disability historian explained:

> The words we use to define problems, or to evaluate potential solutions to those problems, structure thinking by linking concrete situations to moral categories. Section 504 transformed federal disability policy by conceptualizing access for people with disabilities as a civil right rather than as a welfare benefit.[53]

It is clear from this example that the executive branch, with its rule-making authority, has a potent role in making enforceable legal policy.

Judicial Process: Interpretation and Application

The third branch of government, the judicial branch, has the ultimate power to make or mold law. Judges identify, interpret, and apply statutes and regulations; and in the absence of statutory law, they determine and apply common law principles and precedents. This means that courts are also law-making agencies. Furthermore, judges have the power to overturn legislation or regulations if they decide that the original statute was not properly authorized or considered, or if they decide that the executive agency has erred or overstepped its authority in issuing regulations.

Unlike the other two law-making branches of government, courts can act only in very limited circumstances: a factual dispute or controversy has been raised between two parties, or a government has initiated a specific criminal prosecution or regulatory enforcement proceeding. This narrow focus affects the ability of a court to make a comprehensive, policy-based decision. Judges are constrained to consider only the specific facts and issues raised by a particular controversy. They only consider facts relevant to the specific issues raised in a case, and in the vast majority of cases, they only hear argument and analysis from the parties to the case. These arguments are often couched in stark black-and-white terms. By contrast, legislatures and agencies hold public hearings and take testimony from any interested member of the public or special interest group.

This focus can lead to narrow judicial decisions or language in one decision that does not fit easily with the controversies in another decision under the same statute. For example, a disability case involving a plaintiff who uses a wheelchair and has mobility impairments raises very different issues from a case involving a deaf person, who does not need many alterations in the physical work environment but who does need alterations in communication methods. Similarly, a person with developmental disabilities may not need environmental or communication changes, but may need alterations in job duties and supervision. Nevertheless, decisions issued in a wheelchair case will often be applied in other contexts, and vice versa. A deaf plaintiff may seek a sign language interpreter as a remedy for discrimination by a university. If the judge's decision ordering the university to "provide" deaf students "sign language services" is not written broadly enough, it may create real problems for the next deaf plaintiff, who may not use sign language and needs CART (computer-assisted real-time transcript) technology.

Even though a decision is binding on only two parties, it can have widespread effect under the doctrine of *stare decisis*. A judicial decision will be applied to similar facts in similar controversies within the same jurisdiction, unless an appeals court overturns the decision. Decisions by courts of appeals apply to all similar controversies within the multistate circuit. Only the decisions of the U.S. Supreme Court are binding on all federal courts, regardless of jurisdiction.

A particular law may have different interpretations and applications in neighboring states. The ADA has been challenged and invalidated for certain purposes by some of the courts of appeals. For example, in *Erickson v. Board of Governors*, the U.S. Court of Appeals for the Seventh Circuit ruled that Congress did not have authority under the Constitution to prohibit employment discrimination with respect to state employees.[54] This means that state employees cannot sue the state for monetary compensation for injuries suffered as a result of discrimination. Imagine two deaf state employees who have not received weekly interpreter services for staff meetings. As a result, they have missed crucial information, cannot collaborate with other employees, and have received unsatisfactory evaluations. They have been forced out of their state jobs, and they each seek to recover compensation for discrimination. A victim of such discrimination in Tennessee might be able to recover monetary compensation, but a victim in Illinois would be out of luck. Courts in the U.S. Court of Appeals for the Seventh Circuit (which includes Illinois) will no longer allow this claim.

This lack of uniformity in federal law is hugely frustrating and confusing for the public to understand. The Supreme Court will sometimes take issues under consideration when the courts of appeals have conflicting interpretations. The holding in *Erickson* became a uniform national policy in 2001, when the Supreme Court decided *Board of Trustees of Univ. of Alabama v. Garrett*. The Court ruled that the ADA does not authorize employment lawsuits for damages against any state government. Now, deaf and disabled individuals are unable to bring such suits, regardless of where they live.

The other significant difference in judicial lawmaking is that a judicial decision is initially the work of one individual, the trial judge. If a ruling is appealed, the opinion of the trial judge is reviewed by a very small number of individuals. In the federal courts, a three-judge panel at the circuit court level reviews the opinion of a district judge. If the case is appealed further to the Supreme Court, only nine justices review the case. The usual practice is for one judge to author a decision, and the other judges to sign on to that opinion.[55] As a result, an individual judge can often frame and articulate a decision using language choices that are personal and distinctive. This is a very different process from the multi-level, multiperson, debate-and-consideration process in Congress or the executive agencies. Whereas a legislature or agency may seek a compromise position to please the largest percentage of the public, judges have no such motivations. Because they have the last word, judges do not need to mediate or participate in give-and-take.

THE MEANING OF *EQUALITY*

Democracy depends on a commitment to the concept of equality, since all votes are deemed to be equal in choosing political leadership and establishing political policy. Our earliest political document, the

Declaration of Independence, includes the central tenet that "all Men are created equal."

However fundamental this concept is to our national psyche, there is surprisingly little agreement on what the word *equal* means. Neither the Constitution nor the Bill of Rights even mention equality or equal rights, much less define their meanings. It is clear in retrospect that the concept was understood in the context of the social and political climate of the time. "All Men" did not include either women or people of African heritage. In fact, the Constitution was specifically interpreted to permit slavery in 1857. In the infamous *Dred Scott* case, Chief Justice Taney ruled for the Supreme Court that citizenship was available only to white persons born in the United States and to legal immigrants who were naturalized citizens.[56]

Equal Protection of the Laws

It was not until the end of the Civil War, when Congress passed the Civil Rights Act of 1866, that the concept of racial equality was written into federal law. That act declared that "all persons, of every race and color, and without regard to previous condition of servitude" shall have the "same rights."[57] The actual term *equal protection of the laws* did not appear in our formal code until the 1868 ratification of Section 1 of the Fourteenth Amendment to the Constitution, which had the effect of overturning the *Dred Scott* decision.

> Section 1. All persons born or naturalized in the United States, and subject to the jurisdiction thereof, are citizens of the United States and of the state wherein they reside. No state shall make or enforce any law which shall abridge the privileges or immunities of citizens of the United States; *nor shall any state* deprive any person of life, liberty, or property, without due process of law; nor *deny to any person within its jurisdiction the equal protection of the laws*. (Emphasis added.)

Nonlawyers are often surprised to find that the Fourteenth Amendment right to equal protection applies only to any *state*. By its terms, this language does not prohibit discrimination by private citizens. The Equal Protection standard has also been extended to the federal government under the Fifth Amendment.[58] The Equal Protection standard essentially directs federal and state governments to treat all similarly situated persons alike.

The Equal Protection Clause is a good example of a legal standard that is amorphous or protean in nature. The Fourteenth Amendment itself does not define the term equal protection of the laws.[59] Succeeding statutes passed by Congress and subsequent interpretations by the Supreme Court have developed the meaning of the phrase *equal protection*. From an historical perspective, it is obvious that the Fourteenth Amendment, ratified in 1868, was adopted to protect the interests of freed slaves and citizens of African heritage in the aftermath of the Civil War.

However, the laws of our governments distinguish between groups of people in ways that are now seen as discriminatory even though they do not employ overtly racial classifications. After racially discriminatory voting laws were struck down, southern states responded with laws that denied the vote to people who could not pay a special poll tax. The poll tax laws do not mention race; they apply only to people who do not have enough money to pay the tax. This was only a subterfuge. The poll tax laws had an indirect discriminatory impact on recently freed slaves and poor black sharecroppers in southern states, resulting in the same result as an overt racial standard. Does a law that distinguishes between people on the basis of their wealth violate the Equal Protection Clause?

Other southern states adopted literacy requirements for voters. Southern legislators justified the literacy standards on the basis that a person who cannot read newspapers might not be considered informed about public issues and candidates. Black citizens in the southern states were routinely excluded from public schools or given extremely inferior funding for their schools. As a result, black people attempting to vote could not pass the literacy tests. Furthermore, the tests were often applied selectively. An illiterate white voter would not have to demonstrate literacy. A black voter might be required to read and interpret difficult legal passages in order to register to vote. Do literacy laws violate the Equal Protection Clause?

Laws make many other distinctions between people that are not based on race. Women could not vote, serve on juries, or even hold property in some states. A law in Nebraska prohibited schools from teaching a foreign language to students below the eighth grade. State and local governments enforced housing covenants and provided scholarships to public universities that were limited to Christians.

Laws against people with disabilities were also common, going back to the Roman Code of Justinian, which denied deaf people the ability to hold and control property, make contracts, or write a valid will.[60] In most states, deaf people could not serve on a jury.[61] Under common law rules, they were not permitted to testify as a witness or party in a trial (on the basis of the assumptions that deaf people were of limited intelligence and could not communicate effectively enough to understand the court proceedings or take the oath to tell the truth).[62] Laws also prohibit blind people from holding a driver's license, and state laws have required deaf people to drive cars equipped with extra mirrors. Do any of these legal classifications violate the language or spirit of the Equal Protection Clause?

Rational Basis for a Classification

The interpretation of the Equal Protection mandate has been extremely fluid in the hands of the Supreme Court. When a state or federal law makes distinctions between groups of people, the Court is sometimes asked to rule on whether the classification violates the Equal Protection Clause. The general rule is that legislation is presumed to be valid and will be sustained if the classification drawn by the statute is rationally related to a legitimate state interest.[63] Under the traditional Equal Protection approach, legislatures are given the power (known as *discretion* by legal writers) to establish classifications and to treat people differently to carry out legitimate government economic and social policies. There is a strong presumption that most acts of government are constitutional. As long as the Court is able to find that a state has any rational basis for the law, the law will be upheld. For example, the state law denying a driver's license to a blind person would clearly be upheld. A state law denying a driver's license to a deaf person would not be upheld because there is no rational basis for it. But the law requiring the extra mirrors might be found valid if the legislature can articulate a reason for it. The presumed safety benefit of assuring that a deaf driver has additional visibility would probably be sufficient. In normal legal analysis, the statute will get the benefit of any doubt, and the state law will be upheld.

In the context of disability law, no case is more stark than that of Carrie Buck, a developmentally disabled woman who was involuntarily sterilized by the state of Ohio because of the assumption that her children would also be developmentally disabled. Ms. Buck's lawyers argued that state-imposed sterilization, against her will, on the basis of disability, was not constitutional. In *Buck v. Bell*, the Supreme Court disagreed. Judge Oliver Wendell Holmes ruled that persons with disabilities were "a menace" to society and would "sap the strength of the state."[64] In an infamous dictum, he declared, "Three generations of imbeciles are enough." The Court clearly believed that there was a rational basis for the state law permitting involuntarily sterilization of persons with disabilities.

Suspect Classifications

Judges will not be so deferential when a statute classifies people on the basis of race, alienage, or national origin. The Court has held that classifications based on race are "suspect" and therefore will be subjected to heightened or "strict" scrutiny. The Court will not look with generosity and benignity on these state laws. Laws that do not treat people equally on the basis of race, alienage, or national origin will be struck down unless there is a compelling state interest that the law is intended to protect.

For example, marriage laws are generally under the authority of states, and a federal court will ordinarily not interfere with state marriage laws. A Virginia statute was typical of southern anti-miscegenation statutes, which prohibited marriages between "white" and "colored" persons. Virginia prosecuted Richard and Mildred Loving for violating this statute by marrying and living in Virginia as husband and wife. The Court examined this statute in 1967 in the case of *Loving v. Virginia*.[65] The Commonwealth of Virginia argued that the state law was "equal" since both the black person and the white person were subject to equal punishment. Under traditional rules of equal protection, the Commonwealth of Virginia also justified its law on the grounds of tradition and the desirability of racial purity. However, under the strict scrutiny standard appropriate to a racially based classification, the Supreme Court invalidated the Virginia statute (and by extension, the statutes of sixteen other states that prohibited miscegenation).

There are very few legitimate justifications for a law that discriminates on the basis of race or national origin. Racial classifications are permissible to remedy school desegregation, in which children are assigned to schools by race. However, these plans are only upheld when they are part of a plan to overcome past discrimination. One of the few occasions in which the Court has upheld a racial classification that penalizes a racial minority was *Korematsu v. U.S.*[66] Concentration camps were established on the West Coast during World War II. American citizens of Japanese ancestry were ordered to leave their homes and report to "assembly centers." The Court ruled that these military orders were justified to prevent espionage and sabotage, due to the wartime situation of "direst emergency and peril," with an enemy "threatening our shores."

In situations that are not so dangerous, laws that classify by race or national origin are usually struck down. The Court has stated that race, alienage, and national origin are

> [s]o seldom relevant to the achievement of any legitimate state interest that laws grounded in such considerations are deemed to reflect prejudice and antipathy—a view that those in the burdened class are not as worthy or deserving as others. For these reasons and because such discrimination is unlikely to be soon rectified by legislative means, these laws are subjected to strict scrutiny and will be sustained only if they are suitably tailored to serve a compelling state interest.[67]

In the 1920s, a Nebraska statute prohibited teaching children younger than eighth grade in any foreign language. The legislature was acting in hostility to German immigrants after World War I and especially to the insular nature of some immigrant families which were not assimilating into mainstream American culture. A young teacher named Meyer was arrested for teaching in German in a private Lutheran school. The Nebraska court upheld his conviction and ruled that this law was justified by the traditional state "police power" to protect the safety of the country, stating:

> The Legislature had seen [that] . . . to allow the children of foreigners, who had emigrated here, to be taught from early childhood the language of the country of their parents was to rear them with that language as their mother tongue. It was to educate them so that they must always think in that language, and, as a consequence, naturally inculcate in them the ideas and sentiments foreign to the best interests of this country. The statute, therefore, was intended not only to require that the education of all children be conducted in the English

language, but that, until they had grown into that language and until it had become a part of them, they should not in the schools be taught any other language. The obvious purpose of this statute was that the English language should be and become the mother tongue of all children reared in this state. The enactment of such a statute comes reasonably within the police power of the state.[68]

The Supreme Court disagreed, however, and struck down this law because it violated the Fourteenth Amendment, saying:

The protection of the Constitution extends to all, to those who speak other languages as well as to those born with English on the tongue. Perhaps it would be highly advantageous if all had ready understanding of our ordinary speech, but this cannot be coerced by methods which conflict with the Constitution.[69]

The Court noted that the Nebraska legislature generally has full authority to regulate its schools, the conduct of teachers, the mandatory curriculum, and methods of instruction. Ordinarily, a federal court would never strike down a state statute on these matters. Furthermore, the Court acknowledged that Nebraska had a legitimate interest in fostering community spirit and a sense of loyalty, American citizenship, and identification by encouraging the use of English by immigrant children.

However, in this situation, Nebraska was denying essential student and teacher rights on the basis of membership in a specially protected group (persons who speak a foreign language, persons who were born in a foreign country). Since the state could not show actual harm from allowing immigrant families to maintain their home language, a law forbidding foreign language teaching was not permissible. In this case, the right of equal protection meant that those who wished to learn differently, in a different language, received Fourteenth Amendment protection.

This case has some fascinating potential application to deaf children, whose parents could certainly argue that their children have an Equal Protection right to learn in their natural, visual language, ASL. In the days when many school systems offered only oral deaf education programs, there were advocates who considered using the *Meyer* case to challenge the practice under the Equal Protection Clause. However, lawyers have never felt that this approach would succeed in the courts. Unlike race, alienage, or national origin, deafness is simply not recognized as a classification that is entitled to special protection under the Fourteenth Amendment. Faced with an Equal Protection challenge to oral-only deaf education, a court would be most inclined to uphold the school system. Statutes such as the Individuals with Disabilities Education Act (IDEA) are much more likely than the Equal Protection Clause to be successful in challenging an oral-only education system.

Legislative classifications based on gender have been found to be "inherently suspect and must therefore be subjected to close judicial scrutiny."[70] The Court recognizes that gender is not usually a sensible ground for differential treatment: "[W]hat differentiates sex from such non-suspect statutes as intelligence or physical disability . . . is that the sex characteristic frequently bears no relation to ability to perform or contribute to society."[71] In *Frontiero v. Richardson*, the Court struck down the rules for military benefits for dependents. Male military personnel could always receive benefits for their wives as their dependents. Female military personnel could only get these benefits for their husbands if they could prove that their husbands were, in fact, dependent on them for support. The military rationalized this on the assumption that few men were actually dependent on their wives, whereas most wives were dependent on their husbands, and therefore the government would save money by making these assumptions. The Court ruled that these assumptions were based on outmoded and degrading stereotypes that violated the Equal Protection Clause. Gender, like race and national origin, is an immutable characteristic determined solely by the accident of birth. Therefore, distinctions based solely on gender must be given strict judicial scrutiny to see if they are legitimate under the Equal Protection Clause. In most situations, men and women should receive precisely identical treatment under the law.

Unlike the Nebraska case, where children were being taught in a different, minority language, the primary Equal Protection cases involve minority children who wish to learn in exactly the same way and in the same facilities as the white majority. After the Civil War, southern states developed a system of parallel segregated white/black facilities. Black Americans might receive nominally identical services, but in physically separate facilities. For example, black children and white children were both entitled to public school education, but in physically different schools. In practice, the black facilities were significantly inferior and inadequately funded and staffed. Both black and white people were entitled to public transportation, but black seating was literally in the back of the bus, and black riders could be denied carriage if no "black" seats were available. Black persons were entitled to health care, but in vastly inferior wards or hospital facilities.

The Supreme Court upheld this system of legal segregation in 1896 in the decision of *Plessy v. Ferguson.*[72] *Plessy* was not an education case; it involved railway transportation. Louisiana law prohibited any "colored" person from sitting in a railway car with "non-colored" passengers and established a system of "separate, but equal" seating. The Supreme Court held that segregated seating was constitutional as long as equal facilities were available to non-Caucasian passengers. According to the Court, "A statute which implies merely a legal distinction between the white and colored races—a distinction which is founded in the color of the two races, and which must always exist so long as white men are distinguished from the other race by color—has no tendency to destroy the legal equality of the two races."[73]

The Court also went on to say:

The object of the [Fourteenth A]mendment was undoubtedly to enforce the absolute equality of the two races before the law, but, in the nature of things, it could not have been intended to abolish distinctions based upon color, or to enforce social, as distinguish distinguished from political equality, or a commingling of the two races upon terms unsatisfactory to either. Laws permitting, and even requiring, their separation, in places where they are liable to be brought into contact, do not necessarily imply the inferiority of either race to the other, and have been generally, if not universally, recognized as within the competency of the state legislatures in the exercise of their police power. The most common instance of this is connected with the establishment of separate schools for white and colored children, which have been held to be a valid exercise of the legislative power even by courts of states where the political rights of the colored race have been longest and most earnestly enforced.[74]

The Court ruled that Louisiana was acting reasonably in segregating the races, because of the established usages, customs, and traditions of its people, as well as the preservation of "public peace and good order." The Court did not examine the condition of the railway cars to see if they were in fact equal. The Court was satisfied that as long as both races have equal civil and political rights, they can be physically separated.

Only one dissenter, Justice John Harlan, was willing to look behind this pretext of equal services to acknowledge that the true purpose of the legislation was to keep black passengers in separate and inferior accommodations, without contact with white passengers. Justice Harlan asserted that "[o]ur constitution is color-blind, and neither knows nor tolerates classes among citizens. In respect of civil rights, all citizens are equal before the law. The humblest is the peer of the most powerful."[75] He understood that the putative equality of segregated train cars was a pretense for racial dominance. His view would not be accepted for years.

The doctrine of separate, but equal was not unmasked until the 1954 unanimous Supreme Court decision in *Brown v. Board of Education.*[76] The Court ruled that segregation by race in state public schools, pursuant to state laws permitting or requiring such segregation, "denies to Negro children the equal protection of the laws guaranteed by the Fourteenth Amendment—even though the physical facilities and other 'tangible' factors of white and Negro schools may be equal."[77] Essentially, the Court concluded that "[i]n the field of public education the doctrine of 'separate but equal' has no place. Separate educational facilities are inherently unequal."[78] Segregated public schools are not equal, and cannot be made equal, even if a state provides substantially equal funding, buildings, resources, and staff to both school systems.

Equality for one group of Supreme Court justices is clearly not equality for all time. The Supreme Court not only has the last word in interpreting the Constitution, but it can also change its mind. In *Brown*, the Court expressly overruled its earlier decision in *Plessy v. Ferguson.* The *Brown* decision quoted contemporary psychological studies (as opposed to legal arguments) on the nature of social inferiority and segregation. It belittled the state of psychological knowledge at the time of the *Plessy* decision. More controversially, the Court stated that the history of the Fourteenth Amendment is inconclusive as to public education, and that its decision was reached in the light of the full development of public education and its present place in American life, not on conditions when the Fourteenth Amendment was adopted.

Brown established a standard of rights that must be available to all "on equal terms." Enforcing this right was another matter, requiring the intervention of the legislative and executive branches of government. Following ten years of protests, political shenanigans, and civil disobedience, Congress passed the Civil Rights Act of 1964, with a straightforward proposition: It is against the law to discriminate on the basis of race, color, religion, sex, or national origin.[79] This law, and subsequent case law, established the vital principle that it is illegal to discriminate on the basis of characteristics irrelevant to job performance. Denial of access to public accommodations and public services based on race or religion is also, simply, unconstitutional.[80] But this act only protects specific, enumerated groups. The Civil Rights Act of 1964 does not mention disability or handicap.

EQUAL PROTECTION APPLIED TO DISABILITY

Is Disability a Suspect Classification?

Many disability advocates were hopeful that disability would come to be considered a suspect classification, entitled to special protection under the Constitution.

The Supreme Court finally addressed the issue in *City of Cleburne, Texas v. Cleburne Living Center.*[81] A group home for people with developmental disabilities attempted to locate in a residential neighborhood. The city required the group home to seek a special use permit for a "hospital for the feeble-minded," and then denied them the permit. The group home sued, saying that the city's zoning ordinances discriminated against them on the basis of disability by denying them the right to live in the neighborhood, even though boarding houses and hospitals were permitted.

The Supreme Court had several possible approaches to decide this case. The district court judge had ruled that the zoning ordinance was constitutional because it was justified by legitimate fears of neighbors about their safety and the number of developmentally disabled people who would be living in the group home. The judge gave the ordinance the minimal level of judicial scrutiny. As usual, he deferred to the judgment of the legislature because there was a rational basis for the ordinance. The Supreme Court could have upheld this decision.

The plaintiffs argued that by limiting the housing rights of persons with disabilities, the city was creating a suspect classification. As a result, they asked the court to use the strict level of judicial scrutiny and strike down the ordinance. The Court could have adopted this reasoning.

The U.S. Court of Appeals for the Fifth Circuit took an unusual approach when it upheld the zoning ordinance on appeal. That court ruled that people with developmental disabilities constituted a "quasi-suspect" classification, and that the courts should use an intermediate level of scrutiny. In other words, there can be legitimate reasons for a government to treat people with developmental disabilities differently from other people. However, the court would only uphold the classification if the government had a "substantial" interest in treating these people differently. The Fifth Circuit judges compared developmental disabilities to gender and illegitimacy. These groups have also been granted quasi-suspect status, because they are characterized by immutable (permanent) conditions beyond their control, present from birth, which are readily identifiable and that tend to subject the members of the group to opprobrium and irrational legal, social, and political limitations. The Supreme Court could have ruled that people with mental disabilities were in a quasi-suspect classification.

Instead, the Supreme Court chose a fourth solution. First, it refused to grant persons with mental disability any heightened judicial review (strict scrutiny). Developmental disability is not a suspect classification. However, the Court did find that the city had violated the Equal Protection Clause. The Court ruled that there was no reason for the city to require the permit, except for irrational prejudice against people with mental disabilities. In this case, the group home in question was small, closely supervised, and highly regulated. It presented no danger or inconvenience to the neighborhood. Denying the home a permit was irrational.

The Court's opinion reveals its belief that people with mental or physical disabilities are, in fact, different from people without disabilities, and that there are times when different treatment is appropriate and necessary. Although a special permit was not necessary or rational in this case, the Court recognized that persons with developmental disabilities have a "reduced ability to cope with and function in the everyday world."[82] Therefore, there are circumstances where it is appropriate for a legislature to treat them differently.

The Supreme Court stated that a legislature is better equipped than any court to determine how to handle the diverse needs of people with disabilities. The Court cited Section 504 and education laws to show that Congress is acting properly to secure the rights of people with disabilities, so that courts do not have to intervene. The Court admitted that these laws sometimes provide a lesser degree of services than that given to others. For example, children with disabilities are guaranteed only an "appropriate" education rather than an "equal" education. However, the justices were not willing to upset legislative decision making where it appears to have been rational, saying, "Especially given the wide variation in the abilities and needs of the retarded themselves, governmental bodies must have a certain amount of flexibility and freedom from judicial oversight in shaping and limiting their remedial efforts."[83]

The *Cleburne* case was disappointing for the disability community, even though the Court did allow the group home to be established. In *Cleburne*, the Supreme Court was saying that the highest degree of equal protection is not always appropriate for people with disabilities, because there is enough that is different about people with disabilities to justify certain kinds of different legislative treatment. The Court also pointed out examples in which government has extended special educational and vocational rights and benefits to people with disabilities, which are not available to people who are not disabled. This suggested to the Court that treating people with disabilities differently could be legitimate under the Constitution.

Also, since developmental disabilities and some physical disabilities do have a real, measurable effect on the person's abilities to learn, to live independently, and to work, the Court seemed to accept the lower degree of judicial scrutiny for laws that would otherwise appear to be discriminatory. By contrast, the Court could think of almost no situation (other than remedying past discrimination) that would justify different treatment in schools or on the job for people of different races or national origin, saying, "[Race and national origin] are so seldom relevant to the achievement of any legitimate state interest that laws grounded in such considerations are deemed to reflect prejudice and antipathy."[84]

When *Equal* Means *Unequal*

Equal Protection analysis is also complicated by the nature of the remedy for discrimination. In race cases, the remedy for discrimination is equal treatment. African American or other minority students must be admitted to universities in a color-blind manner. Efforts to provide special treatment such as special recruitment plans are regularly struck down by the courts as impermissible "affirmative action," despite their laudable intent.

In the context of disability, the idea of equal treatment has a completely different, almost opposite, meaning than discrimination based on race. Ironically, there are many situations where strictly equal treatment of a person with a disability and a person without a disability will result in substantial denial of opportunity. Two classic examples will demonstrate the problem.

A student in a wheelchair who meets the school's entrance standards has a legal right to enter any classroom for her classes. The student is being treated identically to students who can walk. However, if her classroom is on the second floor, it is not accessible to this student. The student is physically unable to reach or enter the classroom, even though no school rule or law keeps her out. The equal treatment is inherently unequal in its effect on her. For her to have an equal opportunity to participate in the school's educational program, the school will have to treat her differently from other students, perhaps by relocating her classes to a ground floor classroom or by ensuring that any building she must enter is equipped with ramps or elevators.

Similarly, a deaf student who meets entrance standards also has a legal right to enroll in any class in a university. The student is not being denied equal treatment under standard nondiscrimination analysis. However, the lecture and class discussion are virtually useless to him. Again, strictly equal treatment has a discriminatory effect on this student. Although he receives exactly the same lecture and discussion available to every other student in the class (equal treatment), he does not have equal opportunity to learn and participate in the curriculum.

In the context of disability, equal opportunity often requires unequal, special treatment, such as spending money for ramps, elevators, interpreters, and other accommodations and modifications. This conundrum has created many headaches for disability lawyers trying to fit disability into the traditional framework of Equal Protection law.

Claire Ramsey has documented the "ideological trap" of assuming that all children are created equal when deaf and hearing children are educated together in a mainstreaming environment.[85] For a year, she closely observed classroom interactions and educational services in a regular public elementary school. Three profoundly deaf second-graders spent part of their days in a self-contained classroom for deaf and hard of hearing students. For part of the day, they were mainstreamed with 20 hearing children in a second-grade classroom with a sign language interpreter/instructional aide. In the self-contained classroom, the deaf students were seen as children who needed a specialized, often innovative, kind of teaching "because they were deaf."[86] In their mainstream classroom, however, they were defined as "children who merely needed their civil right to educational access ensured."[87] The regular teachers firmly believed that the deaf students were receiving equal access to educational services because of the presence of an interpreter in the regular classroom.

In this mainstream setting, teachers often failed to provide special adjustments for the deaf students. For example, Ramsey notes that hearing teachers would direct all the students to look at their textbooks during a lecture, and that a deaf child who continued to watch an interpreter was considered disrespectful, inattentive, or disobedient. In the cafeteria, all the children were directed to sit along one side of a long table, with no one across from them. Side-by-side seating greatly minimizes the ability of a deaf child to communicate with peers. When deaf children received permission to sit with each other, rather than in the next available seat, there was great resentment and accusations of favoritism and enjoying extra privileges. Hearing children and teachers interpreted the students' trips to an audiology clinic for hearing tests as "extra field trips." Teachers also resented the low student–teacher ratio in the deaf students' self-contained classes. Any different or extra treatment at all was seen as "pampering" or the giving of a special privilege, rather than accommodation for the differences created by deafness.[88] According to Ramsey, "The ideal of equality is not sufficient in itself to help teachers differentiate between the crucial differences that deaf children present in the classroom from the many ways that they appear to be like other children."[89]

In disability cases, unlike race cases, special, unequal treatment *is* necessary, because equal treatment does not provide equal opportunity. Under Equal Protection analysis, there is a great danger that a court might conflate (impermissible) affirmative action with (permissible) reasonable accommodation. Traditional Equal Protection analysis does not provide lawyers and judges with the linguistic tools to make these distinctions easily.

STATUTES ATTEMPTING TO ESTABLISH EQUAL PROTECTION FOR PEOPLE WITH DISABILITIES

Disability advocates have been very successful in using statutes and legislative action, rather than court cases, to address equal protection by building on the traditional government function of social welfare. The original statutes establishing rights for people with disabilities took the form of granting benefits. Under numerous vocational rehabilitation acts, beginning with the Smith-Fess Act in 1920, people with disabilities received substantial benefits for education, training, and job services.[90] The benefits were often called "rehabilitation" services, reflecting their origin in programs for injured war veterans and accident victims who needed rehabilitation to resume their places in the workforce. Veterans from World War I, World War II, the Korean War, and the Vietnam War were the primary beneficiaries. Quickly, however, rehabilitation services were dominated by services to people with congenital or long-term physical and mental disabilities.

The other significant benefit for people with disabilities was the development of the Social Security system. Under Social Security, benefits are available for those who cannot engage in "substantial gainful activity." The Medicaid/Medicare programs also extended health care aid to people with disabilities. Other benefits are available to people with disabilities for housing subsidies, food stamps, and school lunches.

Rehabilitation and social/financial benefits for people with disabilities cannot be squarely placed into standard Equal Protection rhetoric. These programs do not provide equal services. They provide additional services and financial benefits to people with disabilities that are not available to people without disabilities. The controversies within rehabilitation services have generally pitted one disability group against another for limited funding or services (e.g., physical therapy and wheelchairs, special benefits for blind persons, interpreter training programs). Yet, even though the rehabilitation programs provide valuable resources and are intended to be beneficial, participants often perceive them as based on a paternalistic medical model designed to make helpless people with disabilities become "normal," or to support them financially because they never could become "normal."[91]

By contrast, the Civil Rights Act of 1964 was enacted amid a storm of public protest against a history of legislation that was brutally and openly hostile to racial and ethnic minorities. Proponents and opponents of civil rights engaged in confrontational and often violent protests. The resulting Civil Rights Act was written in the context of this battle. It granted proactive, enforceable legal rights of access to "any place of public accommodation," as well as a right to be free from discrimination in employment.

After passage of the Civil Rights Act, the courts developed a body of case law, and the agencies and legislatures enacted further statutes and regulations that became models for disability advocates. However, the act itself was not extended to people with disabilities, and later attempts to amend it were not successful. Senator Hubert Humphrey and Representative Charles Vanik attempted to introduce an amendment in 1972, adding the term *physical or mental handicap* to the list of protected classes in the Civil Rights Act.[92] The amendment received no support from the civil rights community and died without hearings.[93]

Although the ADA is widely cited as a civil rights law, it was derived from a completely different public policy tradition.[94] In the early 1970s, re-authorization of the Vocational Rehabilitation Act was proceeding in an atmosphere of increased need for disability services. Although President Nixon was openly hostile to expanding civil rights, there was still some support for social legislation. The Rehabilitation Act of 1973 expanded the vocational rehabilitation program far beyond its original emphasis on employment, contemplating services to improve "in every possible respect the lives as well as livelihood" of persons served. Most important, it included civil rights language calling for affirmative action in federal employment and employment by federal contractors, removal of architectural barriers, and Section 504:

> No otherwise qualified handicapped individual in the United States . . . shall, solely by reason of his handicap, be excluded from the participation in, be denied the benefits of, or be subjected to discrimination under any program or activity receiving Federal financial assistance.[95]

According to commentators, congressional staff members inserted Section 504 without public debate, late in the deliberative process, eager to ensure that people receiving vocational rehabilitation services would not be denied jobs when they were ready to work. When one staffer "suggested adding a civil rights provision, another staff member hurried out of the room and came back with the wording of Title VI of the Civil Rights Act of 1962."[96] In this way, civil rights language was added without the dangers of amending the Civil Rights Act.[97] As discussed previously, the assignment of rule-making authority to the OCR at HEW, rather than to the Rehabilitation Services Administration, also placed Section 504 firmly in the civil rights tradition established for racial minorities.

However, Section 504 has many limitations. The Rehabilitation Act was enacted under the Spending Clause of the Constitution, unlike the Civil Rights Act, which was enacted under the Equal Protection Clause of the Fourteenth Amendment.[98] Therefore, Section 504 has no general impact on the private sector or the states. It applies only to federal agencies and recipients of federal financial assistance.[99] Theoretically, this is a powerful tool: If the federal government believes that an entity is discriminating against people with disabilities, it will withdraw its support. Federal tax dollars will not be used to support discriminatory acts. Since most hospitals, schools, and universities do receive federal aid, Section 504 cuts a fairly wide swath. But it could not reach most private or commercial enterprises, stores, or restaurants.

Nevertheless, Section 504 was the fulcrum that transformed disability policy from a social service to a civil rights foundation. The newly organized National Center for Law and the Handicapped was established with support from the University of Notre Dame, the American Bar Association, the Association for Retarded Citizens (ARC), and HEW. Their first cases relied on due process and equal protection. But Section 504 immediately provided a new, powerful legal tool. "It seemed like manna from heaven," said founder Robert Burgdorf.[100] Gallaudet University's National Center for Law and Deafness and the National Association of the Deaf's Legal Defense Fund also used Section 504 aggressively and successfully in numerous lawsuits and administrative complaints on behalf of deaf and hard of hearing clients.

Section 504 differs from the Civil Rights Act in one other significant way. The regulations to Section 504 implicitly acknowledge that precisely equal treatment would not result in equal participation opportunities for people with disabilities. Therefore, employers are required to make "reasonable accommodations" for an employee's disabilities, and recipients of federal financial assistance are required to provide "auxiliary aids and services" such as sign language interpreters when needed by a person participating in their programs. Some of these accommodations were expensive or required significant alterations in facilities and procedures. Under the Civil Rights Act, similar requirements might have been seen as affirmative action, which was being struck down regularly by the Supreme Court since the 1978 *Bakke* decision.[101] In *Bakke*, the Court struck down a quota system used by a state medical school to attract qualified minority and women applicants. Proponents of affirmative action argue that to create a color-blind society, it may be necessary for a time to take account of race. The Supreme Court essentially demanded color-blindness in government action, regardless of the benevolent intent. In Section 504, advocates hoped that the obvious differences between people with and without disabilities would be enough to justify different, favorable treatment.

The ADA grew directly from the Civil Rights Act and its traditions. Over the next decade, disability advocates became politically active, making contact and establishing credibility with the civil rights community, the policy makers in Congress, and the executive offices. They became more sophisticated in their knowledge and use of civil rights rhetoric and definitions. Unlike Section 504, the ADA included explicit congressional findings that people with disabilities meet the traditional standard for the heightened judicial scrutiny available to other minorities, using language lifted directly from earlier Supreme Court decisions, such as:

(7) individuals with disabilities are a discrete and insular minority who have been faced with restrictions and limitations, subjected to a history of purposeful unequal treatment, and relegated to a position of political powerlessness in our society, based on characteristics that are beyond the control of such individuals and resulting from stereotypic assumptions not truly indicative of the individual ability of such individuals to participate in, and contribute to, society.[102]

The ADA also states that it was enacted using the authority granted to Congress by the Fourteenth Amendment and the Commerce Clause, which states:

It is the purpose of this Act . . . to invoke the sweep of congressional authority, including the power to enforce the fourteenth amendment and to regulate commerce, in order to address the major areas of discrimination faced day-to-day by people with disabilities. . . .[103]

It is uncertain whether this will be enough to transform disability into a protected status under the Equal Protection Clause. The Supreme Court is not bound by congressional attempts to mandate the scope of constitutional standards.[104] Furthermore, these provisions were inserted without much public debate or congressional consideration. Arlene Meyerson was deeply involved in the drafting and passage of the ADA. She is forthright about the assumptions underlying the law. The drafters conceptualized equal protection as "equal opportunity," which "by necessity required affirmative steps to eliminate barriers to participation." Meyerson explains

> As drafters of the ADA, we never discussed theories of equality. Using the rhetoric of traditional civil rights, which focuses on equal treatment, we incorporated nondiscrimination provisions from section 504 implementing regulations that assured that different treatment would be provided when necessary to achieve equal opportunity.[105]

Subsequent cases have considered, but not resolved, whether the ADA has made laws affecting people with disabilities a suspect or quasi-suspect classification.[106] The case law that follows demonstrates how these assumptions now create problems for people with disabilities bringing discrimination cases in court.

WHO IS PROTECTED UNDER FEDERAL DISABILITY LAWS?

The public and the legal communities have sometimes been confused about who is entitled to protection under federal disability law. Legislators and judges have made some interesting choices in nomenclature and in the definitions they use for disability.

Disabled or Handicapped: A Disability by Any Other Name . . .

Section 504 and the ADA have changed public perceptions about people with disabilities. One proof of this has been in the terminology that is now used to refer to people with disabilities.

In the 1970s, when Section 504 of the Rehabilitation Act was drafted, there was little discussion about the use of *handicapped person* to describe the "beneficiaries" of the law. As discussed above, Section 504 was passed as part of social service legislation, establishing job counseling and job training programs. Patronizing overtones in the word *handicapped* were largely ignored.

This was corrected in 1986, when Section 504 was amended to substitute *individual with handicaps* for *handicapped individual,* and then again in 1992, when *a disability* was substituted for *handicaps.*[107,108] However, the corresponding regulations mostly adopted in 1977 through

1979 have not been amended, probably due to inertia and lack of concerted political pressure on the agencies. For example, the HHS definition states:

> (j) Handicapped person. (1) *Handicapped person* means any person who (i) has a physical or mental impairment which substantially limits one or more major life activities, (ii) has a record of such an impairment, or (iii) is regarded as having such an impairment.[109]

When lawyers write a complaint on the basis of the 504 regulations, they must still describe their client as a *handicapped person*, no matter how the client feels about it.

Almost twenty years later, the drafters of the ADA were more alert to nuance. The ADA protects "individuals with disabilities," and both the statutory and regulatory provisions are consistent.

Who Has a Disability?

The definition of *disability* has been subject to debate and to some recent fine-tuning by courts. The ADA follows the approach of the Rehabilitation Act by giving a functional definition. A disability is a physical or mental impairment that "substantially limits" one or more of the individual's "major life activities."[110] Only a few conditions are expressly ruled out. For example, Congress decided that neither homosexuality nor transvestism are disabilities, nor is current, recent, and unrehabilitated drug addiction. Efforts to exclude coverage of persons with HIV were debated and defeated. Therefore, the remaining definition of disability is very broad.

The business community is unhappy with the uncertain and open-ended nature of this approach. Business owners want to limit the scope of the law, fearing the cost of providing accommodations for millions of people. Also, they would prefer a discrete listing of conditions, specifically vision, hearing, and mobility impairments. They fear the possibility of a business not knowing whether a person is protected by the law until a complaint has been filed.

According to legislators, there was never any serious fight in the Congress over significantly reducing coverage of the ADA.[111] It was not politically expedient to discriminate among disability groups, and it would have been inconsistent with a civil rights bill to protect some, but not other, disability groups. Congress may also have been daunted by the task of drawing lines, because of the huge diversity among the disability community both in terms of type and degree of disability.

Predictably, the broad functional approach has led to litigation. Unlike the days when being labeled *crippled* or *handicapped* was a stigma, many people accept disability status willingly in order to take advantage of the protections in the ADA. Parents are willing to have children classified as *learning disabled* or as having an *attention deficit disorder* in order to benefit from accommodations in educational services and testing under educational disability law. Unresolved issues include the degree of obesity, back pain, infertility, and behavioral disorders such as phobias and anxiety disorders that constitute a disability. Lawsuits have been brought by persons claiming disability on the basis of nearsightedness, high blood pressure, forgetfulness, depression, panic attacks, pregnancy, and disfiguring tooth loss.

For deaf and hard of hearing individuals, defining disability can be semantically and politically problematic. Culturally Deaf people recognize their culture and their language as an important and beneficial part of their identity, not as a "handicap, disability," or "impairment."[112] This is validated in the recent spread of bilingual-bicultural programs for the education of deaf children. People who define themselves as culturally Deaf are not interested in medical definitions of deafness based on hearing loss. Audiologists, on the other hand, use arbitrary and clinically measured increments of decibel loss to determine whether a person is or is not deaf, and further, whether they are classified as having *profound, severe, moderate,* or *mild* hearing loss. Insofar as culturally Deaf individuals choose a sociological or cultural definition of deafness, it is wholly positive. For example, the cultural definition of deafness usually involves the ability to use ASL fluently and having a preference for socializing and marrying within the Deaf community. Degree of clinical hearing loss is seldom an issue in such a definition, and deaf people do not define themselves with reference to any deficiency.

A refusal to see deafness as either pathology or victimhood is psychologically and sociologically healthy. However, it may be legally self-destructive if a person must prove that he or she is disabled to be eligible for civil rights protections. Members of the Deaf community must struggle between using the rhetoric of Deaf Pride and the rhetoric of civil rights. Under the mantle of bilingual-bicultural identity, deafness is not a disability. Under the law as defined by the ADA, it is. A deaf person who experiences discrimination on the job or in school must accept the legal definition of a "substantial limitation" of a "major life activity," with all that this implies, in order to seek reparation or vindication under the law.

A Question of Degree

The question of whether or not a person has a legal disability is, in part, culturally and environmentally determined, and, in part, a question of degree of physical impairment. Even Superman has physical limitations when he is exposed to Kryptonite, but no one thinks he should get a handicapped parking space. The ADA recognizes only those impairments that substantially limit a major life activity.

No conditions are automatically considered disabilities. Instead, on a case-by-case basis, courts look for objective evidence that an individual's life is substantially limited. For example, asthma and allergies are both conditions with a wide range of severity. In a typical case, a court may find that an individual with allergies or asthma is not a person with a disability within the meaning of the ADA (despite a medical diagnosis), because evidence shows that her impairment does not substantially limit her ability to walk, run, work, or engage in other physical activities. The court must make a case-by-case determination about whether respiratory or neurological functioning is, in fact, so severely affected that it impairs a major life activity.[113]

This determination may be affected by environmental and social factors. A person who suffers severely from asthma or allergies in Atlanta, Georgia, may have a difficult time showing equal impairment in Phoenix, Arizona, with its dry environment. A person who has asthma attacks in a textile factory may have no impairment when working in a sterile silicon chip facility.

Many physical impairments are not disabilities under the ADA. Some of the most difficult cases involve back injuries, since such injuries typically involve soft tissues and cannot be medically verified. In the typical case, a person who has experienced a back injury has a medical recommendation not to lift more than a certain number of pounds. Even if the person experiences pain and discomfort, this impairment may not be a legal disability under the ADA if his job does not require lifting. He cannot show a substantial limitation in the major life activity of working. Another individual with identical symptoms may be considered disabled if his age, education, and abilities limit him to manual jobs that he could not perform due to a lifting restriction.[114]

Although people who are deaf or hard of hearing are protected by the ADA, the picture is not so clear when looking at people with temporary, mild, or fluctuating hearing loss, or people whose hearing loss is minimized for most practical purposes with a hearing aid or cochlear implant. In one case, a judge found that an individual with moderate to severe hearing loss in one ear that had lasted for about two years was not disabled under the ADA. Her hearing loss was not considered permanent; it did not have a severe impact on her "functional" ability to hear, and her ability to communicate was not substantially impaired.[115] Judges, like the rest of the hearing population, are not well educated on the realities of hearing and hearing loss. Even mild hearing loss can severely disrupt communication patterns. However, if a person can manage to communicate effectively in spite of deafness or hearing loss, a judge may well find that the person is not entitled to ADA protection.

Furthermore, some disabilities can be cured or successfully overcome with equipment, treatment, or accommodations. Although cancer is considered an impairment under the ADA, an employee who has been successfully treated and is in remission does not have a disability (unless the employer is wary of hiring her because of her history of cancer).[116]

The Supreme Court has recently clarified this issue with a series of cases involving people who had disabilities that were improved significantly by various forms of mitigation. In *Sutton and Hinton v. United Air Lines*, twin sisters applied for jobs as global airline pilots.[117] They were turned down because they both have severe myopia. They sued, saying that they met the minimum standard for visual acuity by using their corrective lenses. The Supreme Court held that they could not bring a case under the ADA because they were not disabled under the ADA. If a person's impairment can be corrected by medication or other measures, he or she has no standing to bring an ADA case. Although the pilots did not get the jobs because of their vision, they are not "disabled" under the law.[118]

This creates a real obstacle for hard of hearing people who are significantly assisted by hearing aids or cochlear implants. Judges without experience in the issue might find that inconvenience in using an aid does not rise to the level of a significant limitation on a major life activity. As a result, the ADA will not avail a hard of hearing plaintiff who is requesting accommodations on the job.

Many people decline to wear hearing aids, knowing that the gain in hearing function they will achieve is marginal or not worth the unpleasant incidental effects of amplification. Other people find that hearing aids benefit them only in limited circumstances. The most appalling outcome of the Court's ruling in *Sutton* is that a judge might find that a plaintiff is not entitled to relief under the ADA if he or she refuses to wear a hearing aid or submit to a cochlear implant.

In a Maryland case, a woman suffering from asthma refused to follow her physicians' recommendations that she take inhaled steroid medication because she feared side effects. The judge ruled that her asthma did not substantially limit her breathing, since the asthma was correctable by medication that she voluntarily refused.[119] But in a comparable case involving hearing, the judge reached a different result. In *Finical v. Collections Unlimited, Inc.*, the plaintiff lost her job as a telephone collector.[120] The employer argued that she could have benefited from hearing aids if she had chosen to wear them; she would not be considered a person with a disability because her impairment would not substantially limit her hearing. The plaintiff testified about discomfort from background noise, but her audiologist had recommended hearing aids. The judge refused to consider whether or not the plaintiff would be disabled if she chose to wear hearing aids. Instead, the judge decided that she should be evaluated "in her current state," which, in her case, meant her ability to hear without amplification. These are lower court decisions, without broad application. They merely illustrate how a judge might approach the issue of disability.

Hard of hearing ADA plaintiffs must be prepared to show proof that hearing aids or cochlear implants do not correct their hearing, or that a refusal to use a device is based on reasonable, rational grounds. Medical evidence itself will not be persuasive and may hurt plaintiffs by showing that a hearing aid does apparently increase their hearing acuity. Plaintiffs must demonstrate the limited effect of hearing aids or implants in actual use (e.g., noisy environments, multiple speakers, or any other circumstances that limit the efficacy of the device in practice).

REASONABLE ACCOMMODATION IN EMPLOYMENT

The word *reasonable* is one of the most flexible terms in law. Whether or not something is reasonable must be analyzed on a case-by-case basis, within a particular social and personal context. What is reasonable for one person, in one setting, may be quite unreasonable for another individual, or in a different context. The ADA and the Rehabilitation Act require employers to make "reasonable accommodations" to known physical or mental disabilities of employees, unless doing so would be an "undue hardship." Typical language is found in Section 501 of the Rehabilitation Act, which applies to federal employees, such as:

An agency shall make reasonable accommodation to the known physical or mental limitations of a qualified handicapped applicant or employee . . . .

(b) Reasonable accommodation may include, but shall not be limited to: . . . acquisition or modification of equipment or devices, the provision of readers and interpreters, . . . and other similar actions.[121]

The requirement to provide reasonable accommodations is the heart of disability law: It is not enough to have a positive nondiscriminatory attitude. It is not enough to treat people with disabilities equally. Instead, an employer may have to take affirmative, positive, and different steps to minimize the effect of an employee's disability and to give that person an equal opportunity to participate and succeed in employment. An employer has a legal duty, in some circumstances, to buy equipment, change procedures, and procure services. This is the great triumph of Section 504 and the ADA.

It is not unique. Employers also have a duty to make reasonable accommodations to the needs of employees on the basis of religion.[122] However, this duty is strictly limited and is not very burdensome on employers. The Supreme Court has ruled that an accommodation would be an undue hardship on an employer whenever the accommodation results in "more than a *de minimis* cost".[123] For example, an employer may have to permit Muslim women to wear hair coverings or other religious garb, but an employer is not required to provide work schedules that accommodate an employee who cannot work on Saturdays for religious reasons. An employer is not required to provide paid time off for religious holidays and ceremonies. That cost would be more than *de minimis*, so it would be an undue hardship on the employer.

Although identical words (*reasonable accommodation, undue hardship*) appear in Section 504 and the ADA, employers have much greater responsibilities. Although employers are not expected to incur undue hardship, they have, at times, been ordered to expend substantial sums for workplace accommodations. The cost of sign language interpreters, for example, can be quite expensive, as can software and reading machines for blind employees or ramps and elevators for people who use wheelchairs. It may be reasonable for a profitable business, no matter how small, to make expenditures for accommodations. A business that is failing or one that is very small, however, is not expected to expend substantial resources on disability accommodations.

Undue hardship is the flip side of *reasonable accommodation*. Under the ADA, the cost of an accommodation is only "undue" if it involves "significant difficulty or expense" when considered in light of factors such as the size of the business operation and the available resources of the employer.[124] It is quite possible, for example, for a business to be expected to provide interpreter services that equal or exceed the salary of the deaf employee who needs them. To an employer, looking at the bottom line of business expenses, being told to hire two people to do one job certainly may appear to be an undue hardship. To a deaf employee, looking at a large and flourishing business enterprise, it will just as certainly appear to be reasonable.

Deafness cases involving reasonable accommodations typically arise when an employee requests interpreters or other communication services and the employer refuses to provide them. The employer may instead ask the employee to communicate in writing, or ask a co-worker with some crude sign skill to interpret. Another typical scenario occurs when a deaf worker is fired or receives a transfer to a less-desirable position. The deaf person alleges that the employer failed to provide adequate communication to enable the employee to perform the job duties satisfactorily. These cases are generally characterized by employer ignorance about effective communication methods with deaf employees and employer concerns about the cost of interpreters.

In one case where these issues were raised, a hard of hearing bookkeeper was transferred to a new position as membership coordinator, a position that involved telephone services. The amplification device on her telephone turned out to be inadequate for her to hear addresses and telephone numbers accurately. She requested a TTY as a reasonable accommodation, but was turned down. Eventually, she was transferred to another position that did not involve telephone duties, and she sued for discrimination. Her supervisor defended the case by claiming that using a TTY would be an undue burden, even though the cost of the service at that time was only $279. He testified that he believed that using a TTY and the state relay service would be too slow and cumbersome, especially since people calling the employee would be unfamiliar with the relay system and would not know how to use it.

The court found that using the relay would be a reasonable accommodation for this employee, because she had produced evidence that the TTY would allow her to do the telephone work her job required. It would allow her to attain an equal level of achievement, opportunity, and participation that a nondisabled individual in the same position would be able to achieve. The judge quoted from part of the legislative history of the ADA that explains the process for determining a reasonable accommodation:

> The reasonable accommodation requirement is best understood as a process in which barriers to a particular individual's equal employment opportunity are removed. The accommodation process focuses on the needs of a particular individual in relation to problems in performance of a particular job because of a physical or mental impairment.

*   *   *

> Having identified one or more possible accommodations, the [next] step is to *assess the reasonableness of each in terms of effectiveness and equal opportunity.* A reasonable accommodation should be effective for the employee. Factors to be considered include the reliability of the accommodation and whether it can be provided in a timely manner.

> [A] reasonable accommodation should provide a meaningful equal employment opportunity. Meaningful equal employment opportunity means an opportunity to attain the same level of performance as is available to nondisabled employees having similar skills and abilities.[125]

The judge then looked at the *undue hardship* question separately. The judge focused on the impact that the accommodation would have, if implemented, on the specific employer *at a particular time.*

This is a multi-faceted, fact-intensive inquiry, requiring consideration of: (1) financial cost, (2) additional administrative burden, (3) complexity of implementation, and (4) any negative impact which the accommodation may have on the operation of the employer's business, including the accommodation's effect on its workforce. The analysis is essentially one of balancing the benefits and the burdens of the proposed accommodation for a particular employer.[126]

The judge was not convinced that using the relay system would slow down the employer's operation unacceptably. He found no evidence that the employee could not handle the volume of expected calls by TTY, even if TTYs operate more slowly than telephones. He also rejected the employer's belief that callers would find the relay system awkward or uncomfortable. The judge characterized these beliefs as inappropriate, patronizing, offensive, and based on the kind of "preconceived discriminatory stereotypes" that the ADA is designed to target.[127] He pointed out that "undue hardship means something greater than hardship. Undue hardship cannot be proved by assumptions nor by opinions based on hypothetical facts."[128]

This intensely factual inquiry is typical of the analysis demanded by the ADA in deafness cases. The standards for physical accessibility are precise, standardized, and based on the inches of clearance in doorways, the heights of sinks, and the loudness and brightness of alarms. But there are no standards for reasonableness or burden of communication methods.

EFFECTIVE COMMUNICATION

The Mandate to Provide Effective Communication

A public accommodation shall furnish appropriate auxiliary aids and services where necessary to ensure **effective communication** with individuals with disabilities.[129] (Author's note: Emphasis added.)

Deaf and hard of hearing people rejoiced to see the requirement in the ADA and in Section 504 that organizations, agencies, and businesses must ensure "effective communication" by furnishing "appropriate auxiliary aids and services." The definition of *auxiliary aids and services* includes qualified interpreters, equipment and devices, or "other effective methods" of making aurally delivered materials available to deaf and hard of hearing people.

This language has produced a revolution in the availability of interpreters, computer-assisted real-time transcription services, and other communication services. The increase in communication services, plus burgeoning technology, has been so rapid and dramatic that not only parents, but older children as well, can tell young deaf children, "When I was your age, we didn't have TTYs, pagers, captioned television, captioned movies, or interpreters available on request in hospitals, courts, schools, or public performances."

A quick review of case law will show many cases where deaf people have successfully argued that they are entitled to interpreter or other communication services. These are lower court decisions or settlements, or in some cases, preliminary decisions in ongoing litigation. They cannot be considered as binding precedent in other situations. However, they illustrate some of the situations where relief has been granted.

- *Connecticut Association of the Deaf v. Middlesex Memorial Hosp.*[130] Twenty-five hospitals joined a comprehensive consent decree to provide sign language interpreters, oral interpreters, and other communication services to patients and companions who are deaf or hard of hearing.
- *Proctor v. Prince Georges Hospital Center.*[131] A deaf man was brought to the hospital after a severe motorcycle accident. Although he and his family repeatedly requested interpreter services, none were provided until, ironically, the day he was discharged. The hospital could not communicate with Proctor well enough to explain to him that his leg had been amputated, nor did they communicate with him effectively when they sought "informed" consent for surgery. The judge ruled that Proctor was entitled to damages under Section 504 because of the hospital's ineffective communication with him at critical times during his treatment.
- *United States v. Board of Trustees of the University of Alabama.*[132] A state university refused to provide interpreter services to a deaf student. The student had previously been turned down by the state vocational rehabilitation agency, which did not approve of the student's career goals. Postsecondary institutions are obligated to provide interpreters and other auxiliary aids and modifications for deaf students who are not recipients of vocational rehabilitation.

- *Gordon v. Harris County.*[133] A deaf person was arrested and brought to the Harris County jail in Houston, Texas. Without interpreter services or a TTY, he could not understand the criminal charges against him or why he was being held. He could not call his family to arrange for bail. The jail has now agreed to provide interpreter services when a deaf person asks for them, to install TTYs, and to make an instructional videotape that will explain in sign language the jail's rules and procedures. It has adopted detailed policies about how to communicate with deaf people held in the jail. In a companion case, the City of Houston agreed to detailed interpreter/TTY policies for the Houston Police Department.

- *Majocha v. Turner.*[134] A deaf parent asked for an interpreter when his young child needed to visit a specialist doctor. The doctor was willing to "take notes" with the father, but refused to provide an interpreter. The doctor's office then cancelled the appointment, telling the parents that he was not willing to see the child at all. The doctor asked the court to dismiss the lawsuit, but the judge refused to do so. The judge ruled that the deaf father had produced credible evidence that a qualified interpreter was necessary for effective communication when the father was discussing surgery on his child.[135]

- *Soto v. City of Newark.*[136] A wedding ceremony performed in a city hall courtroom was a service provided by the city, and the city was ordered to provide interpreter services for a deaf couple so that they could communicate effectively with the magistrate when exchanging their marriage vows.

The DOJ, as well as private deaf litigants and organizations such as the NAD Law Center, have brought cases successfully seeking enforcement of communication rights.

Limitations on the Right to Effective Communication

There are still many complaints in the Deaf community about inadequate interpreter services, telephone services, and captioning. In part, this is due to inherent limitations in the services and technologies themselves. Communication through an interpreter is often flawed, depending as it does on a third party who enables the communication to occur, but also prevents direct one-on-one communication. Interpreted communications can suffer from inaccurate transmission of both language and tone. TTY and relay conversations are much slower than comparable voice communications would be, and both also lose affect and nuance, even when both parties to the conversation are skilled writers and readers. Errors in captioning and real-time transcriptions are legendary and would be comical if people were not depending on the captions for access to television, videos, and movies.

However, much of the dissatisfaction of the deaf community stems from inadequacies in the ADA itself and tepid enforcement by the courts. Some businesses are unaware that the ADA applies to them at all. This is particularly true of professional offices, especially those of lawyers and doctors. Other businesses know about the ADA, but think that it applies only to ramps and physical accessibility issues. They may have no idea that the ADA requires them to provide communication services. For example, fast food restaurants may have curb cuts and accessible bathrooms, but require drive-through patrons to use a remote microphone to place an order before driving up to the window. When a deaf patron drives directly to the window to place an order, the person at the window usually has no idea that the ADA requires the restaurant to modify its ordering policies. The cashier may insist that the deaf person come inside to order.

Many complaints come from people who have received some accommodations, but who felt that the communication was inadequate. In common health care scenarios, a doctor will ask a deaf patient to bring a hearing relative to interpret. If no one is available, the doctor will resort to writing back and forth, even though the patient requests an interpreter. If the patient continues to insist, the doctor may use a staff member who can fingerspell or knows some simple signs. Even if a skilled interpreter is brought in, he or she may not be competent to interpret for this particular patient or in a health care setting. A patient may be uncomfortable and may request a known interpreter who can interpret most effectively for her. Some deaf patients insist on an interpreter certified by the Registry of Interpreters for the Deaf (RID) or the NAD.

All of these complaints are valid for the deaf or hard of hearing individual. Unfortunately, under the ADA and Section 504, there may be no legal remedy for some of these inadequate communications.

COMMUNICATION IS HIGHLY SUBJECTIVE

Communication is a subjective interactive process that is difficult to quantify. Any communication exchange is fraught with potential misunderstanding. The likelihood of misunderstanding is multiplied enormously when the partners to an exchange have different native languages. The likelihood of misunderstanding is greater again when the modalities of communication are different, as between a sign/verbal pair of communicators. Such pairs may have great difficulty achieving understanding, not only of vocabulary and grammar, but also of tone and nuance. Satisfaction with a communication exchange must also be measured from the context of each member of a communication pair. One person may experience an exchange as highly satisfactory and effective, while the other partner to the same exchange may experience frustration and a sense of incomplete understanding.

Deaf individuals and hearing business owners often disagree on the scope of the ADA requirement to provide "effective communication." In the first place, few business people have ever used an interpreter or communicated directly with a deaf person. Myths and assumptions about the ease of learning sign language and the efficacy of speechreading and hearing aids also contribute to misunderstandings about the communication process. In addition, few hearing people understand the challenge of developing competence in written English for a prelingually deaf person. They tend to assume that any literacy skill, however minimal, means that the individual can communicate effectively in writing.

The result is that a deaf person will often experience ineffective communication with a hearing person, while the hearing person does not appreciate the limitations in the communication exchange. Judges are as subject to this tendency as any other person who is not knowledgeable about deafness.

EFFECTIVE COMMUNICATION IS NOT EQUAL COMMUNICATION

Many deaf people interpret the ADA guarantee of effective communication to mean a guarantee of "equal" or "good" communication. In fact, this is another situation where the underlying civil rights paradigm of equality does not fit into the actual language of the ADA. *Effective* communication is actually a fairly low standard that can be satisfied by very minimal understanding and interaction.

The OCR of the HHS has held that the three basic components of effective communication are timeliness of delivery, accuracy of the translation, and provision of communication in a manner and medium appropriate to the significance of the message and the abilities of the individual with the disability. This is a nonquantifiable standard, although it includes an expectation of something called "accuracy." Accuracy also plays a part in determining whether or not an interpreter is "qualified." The DOJ defines a *qualified interpreter* as:

> [a]n interpreter who is able to interpret effectively, accurately and impartially, both receptively and expressively, using any necessary specialized vocabulary.[137]

In practice, however, the skills of an interpreter during a communication have been too elusive for courts to measure.

A troubling line of cases involves deaf drivers who are arrested for traffic violations, such as driving while intoxicated. Often, such arrests occur at night, on weekends, or in dark locations. Because police officers are in a hurry to perform chemical breath tests, there may be little time or inclination to bring in an interpreter. Instead, police officers engage in crude communication involving pantomime of the sobriety field test procedures, written notes scribbled by flashlight, and simply talking, assuming that the deaf motorist can speechread. More than one deaf person has failed the "walk a straight line" test, not realizing that he has been told to walk heel-to-toe.

In *Illinois v. Long*, a court found that communication was effective because the defendant was able to "mimic" the officer who demonstrated the field sobriety test.[138] The judge also believed that the motorist could read written notes and instructions. The Breathalyzer form he was given reads, in part, as follows:

> Considering the above, you are warned: 1. If you refuse or fail to complete all chemical tests request and:
>
> If you are a first offender, your driving privileges will be suspended for a minimum of 6 months; or If you are not a first offender, your driving privileges will be suspended for a minimum of 2 years.
>
> 2. If you submit to a chemical test(s) disclosing an alcohol concentration of 0.10 or more or any amount of a drug, substance or compound resulting from the unlawful use or consumption of cannabis

listed in the Cannabis Control Act or a controlled substance listed in the Illinois Controlled Substances Act and:

If you are a first offender, your driving privileges will be suspended for a minimum of 3 months; or If you are not a first offender, your driving privileges will be suspended for minimum of one year.

Few individuals, hearing or deaf, could decipher this language accurately. However, the judge found that the defendant was cooperative and that his signature on the form showed he was able to communicate effectively by reading and writing, despite his repeated requests for an interpreter. As long as the methods used by the police were effective, the judge held that there was no need to provide the interpreter service requested by the deaf person.

In a case with similar issues, *Nathan v. Anchorage*, police officers testified that Nathan "seemed to understand" what they said to him: He followed their directions and otherwise responded appropriately.[139] When one officer was asked whether he had asked Nathan (in writing) if he could read and write English, he responded, "Nathan nodded affirmatively without hesitation." However, Nathan's former teacher testified that Nathan read at approximately a third-grade level and could not speechread well. Nathan testified that he signed the consent/waiver form only to please or placate the officer, even though he did not understand it. Specifically, he did not understand the word *independent* when he waived his right to an independent blood test. Nevertheless, the trial judge found evidence that convinced her that Nathan could communicate effectively, stating:

Officer Caswell testified that the defendant appeared to be nodding his head "yes" . . . as they were going along. [Nathan facially appeared] to understand what was going on. He was given copies of the forms to read along [as they were being read to him.]

The judge also noted that Nathan had presumably read and studied the state driver's license manual to pass the test and obtain a driving license, and that this was evidence that he could communicate effectively by reading and writing. Even though Nathan might have limited literacy, the judge found:

[T]hat he nonetheless, through life experience, his workplace, the fact that he is a licensed driver, the fact that he does manage to exist and live in a world where deaf people, frankly, are not accommodated many times, tells me that *he most likely understood, at least to the extent that he needed to understand,* that he had a right to an independent test and the other rights that were explained to him on the documents[.] (Author's note: Emphasis added.)

This faulty reasoning by judges indicates that deaf people should not depend on the judicial system to recognize the essential components of deaf communication. The judge is obviously unaware that a profoundly deaf person cannot read along while a form is read out loud, that a deaf person's nod may connote effort rather than understanding, or that a person with a third-grade reading level cannot reliably understand complex and conditional waiver language. For this judge and the appeals court that upheld her decision, the ADA has not changed much in terms of a deaf person's expectation of achieving truly effective communication.

Effective Communication in Health Services

In the area of health care, deaf plaintiffs have been much more successful at demonstrating their need for interpreter services. Perhaps in this area, judges are more likely to be sympathetic to a deaf patient who needs to communicate about health and treatment decisions. ADA and Section 504 regulations and case law recognize that interpreters are required for effective communication with sign language users, although not 100 percent of the time. In part, the need for an interpreter seems to turn on the complexity of the issues to be discussed. The DOJ includes the following example in its ADA manual:

> H goes to his doctor for a biweekly check-up, during which the nurse records H's blood pressure and weight. Exchanging notes and using gestures are likely to provide an effective means of communication at this type of check-up.

> BUT: Upon experiencing symptoms of a mild stroke, H returns to his doctor for a thorough examination and battery of tests and requests that an interpreter be provided. H's doctor should arrange for the services of a qualified interpreter, as an interpreter is likely to be necessary for effective communication with H, given the length and complexity of the communication involved.[140]

In several cases brought by deaf plaintiffs or by the DOJ, hospitals and doctors have agreed to adopt substantial communication policies, covering sign language and oral interpreters, transcription services, assessments of deaf patients, notices to deaf patients of their rights, staff training on how to procure and work with interpreters, agreements on staffing or arranging on-call interpreter services, TTYs and captioned television capability.[141]

There are many cases where deaf plaintiffs have lost cases for hospital interpreter services, but these holdings turn on a peculiarity of the remedies available under Title III of the ADA. Title III does not include a damages (money) remedy for private plaintiffs. The only remedy a deaf person can seek under Title III is a prospective order called an injunction. An injunction does not compensate the plaintiff for past discrimination; it merely orders the defendant to comply with the law in the future. Injunctive relief is only available if the plaintiff can show a "real and immediate threat" of future harm from the defendant.[142] In other words, the plaintiff must be able to prove that he or she will probably use the hospital again and will need to use interpreter services there in the foreseeable future. This has proven to be a very difficult legal hurdle. Mr. Proctor, the motorcycle rider whose leg was amputated, obviously does not plan to be in that hospital again. Courts have shown hostility to expand the impact of the ADA by making very searching investigations of whether a deaf plaintiff has a chronic or recurring condition and whether the hospital is the closest one to the plaintiff's home.

In *Aikens v. St. Helena Hospital*, there was no real dispute that the deaf plaintiff did not get the interpreter services she needed.[143] Her husband was brought in with a massive heart attack, and she needed to consent to surgery and life support decisions. One hospital employee fingerspelled with her for a few minutes before getting frustrated and leaving. Another person gave her a note that her husband was "brain dead." Despite these outrages, she could not get an injunction against the hospital because she could not prove that she would use the hospital again. Her husband had died and no longer needed hospital services, and she herself did not live close to the hospital.

In *Naiman v. New York University*, the court denied injunctive relief even though the patient had visited a particular hospital four times and had been denied effective communication each time.[144] He had shown that the hospital would probably fail to meet his communication needs in the future if he went there again, but he could not show that he would, in fact, need medical services in the future.

Effective Communication in Mental Health Services

Deaf patients' disastrous experiences with mental health services demonstrate the true limits of the guarantee of effective communication. The ADA and Section 504 clearly state that health care services (including mental health care) can be provided to deaf patients through interpreter services. Courts have ordered hospitals to provide interpreters for patients with mental illnesses. However, mental health practitioners must feel great chagrin at these rulings, since most therapists will agree that their services are severely compromised when provided through an interpreter.

In the first place, it is hard to see how mental health counseling can be effective unless the counselor can sign ASL fluently and also is knowledgeable about deafness and its impact on social and family relationships, self-identity, and self-esteem. The social and emotional realities of deafness are an important aspect of the patient's therapeutic needs. A therapist who does not fully understand the patient's culture and use the patient's language will be unable to interpret pathology correctly and unable to provide appropriate therapeutic interventions. Professor Bonnie Tucker has analyzed the issue of communication in mental health services from a legal perspective. She states that to ensure effective counseling of individuals who are deaf, "it is imperative that staff members providing mental health services to deaf patients be able to converse actively with those patients" and that the proposed "remedy" of using sign language interpreters "is totally inadequate to render a solution to the dilemma of providing effective mental health services to the deaf community."[145]

Second, counseling ordinarily depends on a one-on-one therapeutic relationship between the patient and the mental health practitioner. The presence of an intrusive third party, an interpreter, can only interfere with and distort this therapeutic dynamic. The patient and therapist need to communicate directly and openly for therapy to be meaningful. Dependence on an interpreter and the presence of an outsider during therapy may foster feelings of helplessness or shame that will have a negative impact on the therapy. Confidentiality is obviously threatened by the presence of an interpreter, especially in communities where deaf individuals and interpreters see each other frequently.

Third, errors in communication will distort the therapeutic process.

Even if an interpreter is highly skilled (which is often not the case), subtleties of language choice and tone will inevitably be lost or unclear in transmission. In therapy, choices of words or signs may reveal or disguise psychiatric information that is crucial to the therapeutic process.

> The meaning of statements is frequently altered during the translation process, particularly when the interpreter is translating from one language (e.g., ASL) to another (e.g., English). Moreover, because the interpreter is neither a counselor nor skilled in psychological techniques, the interpreter is unable to distinguish between the deaf patient's expressions as linguistic patterns and the patient's true personality responses. As a result, the deaf patient is unable to convey the appropriate message to his or her counselor, rendering the interpreter totally ineffective as a translator.[146]

In spite of these realities, courts continue to order interpreter services in mental health settings. Only one court has recognized that individuals who are deaf require therapists who can communicate with them directly and in their primary mode of communication. In *Tugg v. Towey*, the plaintiffs were patients and family members of patients receiving therapy from a nonprofit agency serving the Deaf community.[147] Interpreters were provided at the agency. But these patients claimed that providing counseling through interpreter services was discriminatory in itself. They asked for services to be provided by counselors who were knowledgeable about deafness and fluent in ASL.

Interpreters and therapists testified that the presence of interpreters hampers counseling and that miscommunication is very likely when translating between English and ASL. The judge discussed the inability of interpreters to sign the word *hallucination* as an example of possible confusion.

In granting a preliminary injunction, the judge found a possibility of irreparable harm to the deaf patients. The agency agreed to hire counselors and psychologists who are deaf and can sign or counselors and psychologists who are knowledgeable about deafness and the Deaf community and have the ability to communicate with clients directly in sign language.[148]

The *Tugg* case is unique, and no other cases have adopted this line of reasoning. As more deaf people enter the field of mental health, other courts might be educated to understand that the only way to provide equally effective mental health services is through therapists who can communicate directly with their patients.

APPROPRIATE EDUCATION AND EDUCATION LAW

Beginning in 1975, the Education for All Handicapped Children Act (now known as the Individuals with Disabilities Education Act, or IDEA) created revolutionary new rights to education services for children with disabilities.[149] This law is a model for studying the creation of law within a process of cultural and social change. It would not have been possible without changes in popular conceptions of *handicaps*, a new culture of protest and political activism, a new "recognition of the importance of public education to integrate disempowered groups into society," and a new perception that individuals with disabilities are members of a minority group who are entitled to protection under civil rights laws.[150]

Access to education is an essential component of the traditional civil rights paradigm. Early civil rights cases analyzed voting rights and access to transportation. But the 1954 decision in *Brown v. Board of Education*, more than any other, excited public opinion and legal scholarship about equal rights. In *Brown*, the Supreme Court recognized that access to education is a cornerstone of democracy, since an educated population is necessary to make informed public decisions. Access to education offers Americans the opportunity to succeed on the basis of merit and achievements.

Today, education is perhaps the most important function of state and local governments. Compulsory school attendance laws and the great expenditures for education both demonstrate our recognition of the importance of education to our democratic society. It is required in the performance of our most basic public responsibilities, even service in the armed forces. It is the very foundation of good citizenship. Today it is a principal instrument in awakening the child to cultural values, in preparing him for later professional training, and in helping him to adjust normally to his environment. In these days, it is doubtful that any child may reasonably be expected to succeed in life if he is denied the opportunity of an education. Such an opportunity, where the state has undertaken to provide it, is a right which must be made available to all on equal terms.[151]

The Supreme Court's reasons for dismantling the southern system of segregated educational facilities were squarely based on sociological research and analysis of the sociological and psychological effects of physical separation of black and white culture.

> To separate [Negro children] from others of similar age and qualifications solely because of their race generates a feeling of inferiority as to their status in the community that may affect their hearts and minds in a way unlikely ever to be undone.[152]

The equal educational rights recognized in *Brown* were not just abstract or theoretical. The Supreme Court ordered the actual physical integration of "separate but equal" race-segregated schools, saying, "We conclude that in the field of public education the doctrine of 'separate but equal' has no place. Separate educational facilities are inherently unequal."[153]

Brown v. Board of Education remains the clearest and most potent expression of nondiscrimination in education. In the years since 1954, changing perceptions of people with disabilities combined with changing perceptions of educational rights that grew from the *Brown* decision. Concepts and language from *Brown* were freely borrowed during the debate and enactment of the original IDEA.[154]

However, despite its powerful precedent in race-based equal protection law, IDEA has been less effective, and its promise has been largely unfulfilled.

> In many states, implementation of IDEA is still incomplete. . . . [H]alf of all children with disabilities, do not receive the educational services their disabilities require. . . . Outcomes of this expensive special education process are also disappointing. One-fourth of students with disabilities drop out of school. More than half of these youths between the ages of fifteen and twenty are unemployed approximately two years after high school. Arrest rates are fifty percent higher for youths with disabilities than for those in the general population. IDEA is a carefully drafted and visionary piece of legislation that has not generated the expected benefits.[155]

The reasons for the disappointing outcome of IDEA can be traced to anomalies in the language of the law, the unique procedure it established for determining the scope of services, and the cultural realities of educational services for children with disabilities, especially deaf and hard of hearing children.

The Guarantee of a Free Appropriate Public Education

IDEA guarantees every child with a disability a "free appropriate public education," which it identifies as:

> Special education and related services that (1) have been provided at public expenses, under public supervision and direction, and without charge, (2) meet the standards of the State educational agency, (3) include an appropriate preschool, elementary or secondary school education in the State involved, and (4) are provided in conformity with the individualized education program.[156]

Special education is defined as "specially designed instruction, at no cost to parents, to meet the unique needs" of a child with a disability.[157] Related services may be required to "assist a child with a disability to benefit" from special education.[158] An individualized education program (IEP) is a written statement designed to address each child's unique educational needs.[159]

None of these definitions include the word *equal*. IDEA actually gives children with disabilities a different right, a right to something called an "appropriate" education, which the law did not define. Most early observers did not seem to notice this, since the original statute and some legislative history were discussed using the rhetoric and language of equal opportunity.[160] Weber noted that the meaning of *appropriate* was so vague that it appeared Congress had left the term completely open to future administrative and judicial interpretation.[161] In the early decisions, courts and commentators assumed that IDEA granted eligible children the right to equal educational opportunity. Some courts ordered whatever services were necessary for students who were disabled to achieve the same educational success as regular education students.

The *Rowley* Decision

Unfortunately, IDEA's potential as a "guarantor of equality" was short-lived.[162] In 1982, the Supreme Court decided the case of a young deaf child named Amy Rowley.[163] Amy entered kindergarten as a bright, eager student. Despite her deafness, she did well in kindergarten because of her intelligence, tutoring from her deaf parents, a good relationship with her kindergarten teacher, and some benefit from hearing aids. However, she missed more than half of what was said in class, and her parents asked for sign language interpreters for her, knowing that her need for communication in the classroom would increase as the curriculum became more demanding.

The Supreme Court took this opportunity to change the popular understanding of IDEA. Instead of ruling that eligible children were entitled to equal educational opportunity, the Court ruled that the law guaranteed only access to public education that was likely to confer "an educational benefit." Instead of equal educational participation, children with disabilities had a right only to a "basic floor of opportunity." The Court declared:

> The intent of the Act was more to open the door of public education to [children with disabilities] on appropriate terms than to guarantee any particular level of education once inside.[164]

The Court ruled that as long as a school district complied with the specific procedures established by IDEA for developing an individual education program, federal courts should not interfere with the professional judgment of educators about the actual educational services that were being provided. The majority of the Court believed that Congress was primarily concerned with the millions of children with disabilities who were receiving no educational services at all. Therefore, the Court ruled that IDEA guaranteed access to minimal educational services, rather than to any particular outcome or degree of opportunity for learning.[165]

The Court was clearly alarmed by the implications of equal educational opportunity for children with disabilities, and therefore it freely interpreted the cryptic phrase *appropriate public education* to be less arduous for the schools. "Whatever Congress meant by an *appropriate* education, it is clear that it did not mean a potential-maximizing education."[166] The Court was also troubled by the logistical difficulties of a standard of equal opportunities for children, which it believed would be an "entirely unworkable standard requiring impossible measurements and comparisons."[167] The Court took a vastly easier route when it ruled that "equal protection" in this act meant merely "equal access" to a basic educational opportunity. However, the Court denied that it was creating any new standard of law:

> Our problem is to construe what Congress has written. After all, Congress expresses its purpose by words. It is for us to ascertain— neither to add nor to subtract, neither to delete nor to distort.[168]

Because Amy Rowley was receiving passing marks and advancing from grade to grade under her IEP, she was receiving an educational "benefit."[169] Even though she could understand less than half of what was said in her classroom, her school district had no responsibility to provide interpreters or to provide other services that would enable her to work to her maximum potential.

1997 Amendments

The *Rowley* case put the brakes on equal educational opportunity case law. Nevertheless, deaf and hard of hearing students were often able to convince courts that they needed placements in schools that used sign language to receive even minimal educational benefits. The Court's directive to judges to defer to the expertise of educational experts was actually a great benefit to deaf children using sign language, due to the emerging professional consensus that deaf children need a visual language context. On the other hand, parents who wrestled with school districts over particular methodologies (ASL, Total Communication, SEE-1, SEE-2, etc.) were unlikely to get a sympathetic hearing from judges.

When Congress revisited this law for reauthorization in 1997, much had changed within the public's awareness and expectations of deafness and other disabilities. Sign language was frequently seen in public events. The high educational expectations of deaf and hard of hearing children were amply demonstrated by public deaf figures such as Heather Whitestone (Miss America 1995) and actress Marlee Matlin, as well as the growing numbers of deaf lawyers, doctors, and entrepreneurs.

The 1997 reauthorization and amendment of IDEA reflected a much more positive view of the educational process. Specifically, Congress made formal findings that it was not satisfied with the current level of educational services available to children with disabilities, saying:

> The Congress finds [that] *improving* educational results for children with disabilities is an essential element of our national policy of ensuring equality of opportunity, full participation, independent living, and economic self-sufficiency for individuals with disabilities.[170]

For deaf and hard of hearing students, there was a greater surprise. IDEA is characterized by a lack of specificity about services. The services appropriate for a particular child with a disability are to be hammered out in an IEP team meeting consisting of parents and school officials. For the first time, however, IDEA was amended to include consideration of a specific educational component that is critically important in deaf education: direct communication. For the first time, the law required the child's IEP team to:

> (iv) consider the communication needs of the child, and in the case of a child who is deaf or hard of hearing, consider the child's language and communication needs, opportunities for direct communications with peers and professional personnel in the child's language and communication mode, academic level, and full range of needs, including opportunities for direct instruction in the child's language and communication mode.[171]

It appears that the Supreme Court's reasoning in *Rowley* now rests on an outdated legislative agenda, since Congress is no longer concerned primarily with children who are completely excluded from school.[172] The current congressional goal is explicitly to improve the services provided to children with disabilities. However, the 1997 amendments did not revise the original definition of appropriate education or expressly overrule the *Rowley* decision. The educational benefit test as expressed in *Rowley* is still with us. However, more demanding IEP procedural requirements have had significant effect. The IEP now requires much more specificity and measurable goals in terms of progress in the general education curriculum.[173] Although the IEP need only confer educational benefit, the expectation of the content of that benefit has been raised to include an expectation of progress and meaningful results. A child's IEP should not be considered sufficient unless it is reasonably calculated to confer measurable educational progress on the basis of the general education curriculum. Essentially, the amendments suggest that the guiding rationale of the law has been elevated from a "basic floor of opportunity" to "meaningful progress."[174]

Procedure and Culture

Several unique features of IDEA are of great interest to sociologists. Although the act establishes a broad federal policy for educational services, IDEA is unusually sensitive to local values, perceptions, and practices.[175] Most laws set up a standard that must be followed. IDEA is different; it sets up a continuing interactive dynamic between parents, teachers, the child, and school officials through an ongoing IEP process. This dynamic is based on an understanding that each child is "unique" and that the school must address this child as an individual. At least once a year, a parent/teacher group sits down as a team to agree on specific educational decisions and plans for a particular child. All participants sign the resulting document.

The IEP team meeting has no counterpart in other civil rights or educational contexts. Parents of a child in a regular fourth-grade classroom have no expectation that they can sit down with their child's teacher to decide on the specific curriculum and method of teaching that will be used with that child. Parents of children with disabilities do have this expectation, and it has created an unusual and often uneasy relationship between parents and schools. As Engel states, "[I]n school districts across the United States, the fate of millions of children with disabilities . . . depends upon the peculiar dynamics of interaction between parents and local educators."[176]

The personal perspectives of each member of the team affect the IEP process, taking into account their personal areas of expertise, biases, values, status, and communication norms. Together, team members must analyze and construct substantive norms for the appropriate education of the individual child. Engel believes that this analysis deliberately blurs the boundaries between law and culture and emphasizes the inseparability of legal processes from the cultural contexts within which they unfold.

The interaction itself is often awkward and unsatisfying. Teachers and administrators are not accustomed to justifying their most minute educational decisions to parents. Often they are struggling with their own limitations in terms of resources and skills. At the same time, they are the professional members of the team and usually understand that role to be one of leadership. Parents are in an unfamiliar world, often the only people around a large table who are not trained in education, psychology, and related disciplines. The educational level of the teacher/ administrator cadre may intimidate them. At the same time, they may feel that they know their child's needs better than the other team members, especially if they too have a disability. Other parents are confused about disabilities and appropriate expectations for their child. Engel has conducted interviews with many parents and explains:

Most parents describe themselves as terrified and inarticulate. Some liken themselves to prisoners awaiting their sentence, and this courtroom imagery emphasizes their perception of the judgmental rather than cooperative quality of the decision making as well as their feelings of vulnerability and disempowerment. . . . Often, but not always, parents feel that their own observations or requests are given little weight and that decisions are based primarily on the recommendations of the professionals. Their own close relationship with the child is viewed as a liability rather than as an asset—a liability that renders their judgments inherently suspect. Some committee chairpersons described with consternation the tendency of the majority of parents to stop attending the annual review meetings after the first few years. Non-attendance is predictable, however, in light of the stress, frustration, and anger expressed by parents in one interview after another.[177]

Deaf parents may experience even more frustration during the IEP team sessions than hearing parents. Although IDEA guarantees parents a right to interpreter services during the meeting, the interpreter is provided by the school system and may be seen as on the school's side rather than a neutral language facilitator. Most of the team members will have had little if any experience in using interpreters, especially in a meeting context. They will make the usual mistakes of referring to or reading from documents, showing overheads or other display language without providing a pause for deaf individuals to read it, and failing to build pauses into the discussion to allow the interpreter to catch up and the deaf participants to interject their own comments. Because school personnel are familiar with the IEP forms or reports and their contents, they often prepare the documents prior to meetings. The deaf parents are expected to read and follow the documents that they are handed during the meeting.

Few parents, deaf or hearing, have mastery of the professional literature and the quantitative testing instruments relied on by the education professionals. The professionals thus tend to devalue parental input, assuming that it is uninformed or erroneous. In social and cultural terms, parental power and authority relative to the other team members is small. In legal terms, however, their power is great, since they can always bring a legal challenge to the team decision. Yet this is a form of power without cultural precedent, and it is often uncomfortable for both parents and educators.

Involving parents in the decision-making process has several theoretical benefits. First, it probably reflects the legislators' belief that this "controlled interaction" was the best format for educational decisions that were both realistic and sensitive to the competing concerns of parents and schools.[178] Second, legislators were probably overwhelmed by the task of creating substantive standards that were appropriate for the vast diversity of disabilities and educational goals for children with disabilities. Third, states and localities were concerned that the federal government would usurp their traditional control over educational policy and planning. By leaving decision making to individual case conferences, Congress left significant control over the shape of educational decisions to the local educational authorities.[179]

Regardless of the interactions and debate that may swirl around an IEP team meeting table, there comes a time when an IEP document is either signed by all the participants, or rejected. If the parties cannot come to agreement, then the controversy is transferred to a vastly different forum. In a court, there is no longer any pretense of discussion, consensus, or agreement. Instead, the decision-making authority is granted to a judge, and the rhetoric often swings from one based on *appropriate* or *reasonable* or *best* to one based on *rights*.

In an instructive case study of *Rowley*, R. C. Smith interviewed virtually all of the parties, lawyers, and judges involved in the litigation, tracing their attitudes and memories at different stages of the case. The role changes that occurred after the Rowley parents filed the first formal complaint set the tone for the years of litigation that followed. The Rowley attorneys initially filed an administrative complaint in the OCR, hoping this would prove to be an informal dispute-settling forum compared with the more threatening atmosphere of a federal lawsuit. School officials and attorneys immediately assumed that they were looking at intransigent parents who were seeking a test case. Both sides ended up hardening their positions, and no settlement was possible.[180]

Parents are traditionally uncomfortable with using a rights analysis. They see themselves in a long-term, continuing relationship with school officials, and they fear jeopardizing goodwill. They also see litigation as a risky strategy that requires huge investments of time, energy, and money. But cooperation is not always possible, and the rights analysis in IDEA provides a tool for the empowerment of children and their parents who are suffering with inadequate and isolating educational services. Engel points out that using a rights analysis also creates a logical trap: Parents want the schools to see their children as learners who need specific adjustments and modifications. But asserting rights to special education services creates a dynamic where these children are seen as "different" and separate from "normal" children.[181]

Just as equal protection may require unequal treatment under the ADA, IDEA sets up the same dilemma: To have a right to an education that offers equal opportunity, a child with a disability must be shown to be so different that a "special" education is necessary. The *Brown v. Board of Education* approach simply does not fit the needs of children with disabilities such as deafness. The *Brown* decision stated that "separate but equal" has no place in education. But for a deaf child to have equal educational opportunities, something separate or different is necessary. Whether it is interpreter services in a mainstream setting or placement in a bilingual-bicultural school that recognizes ASL as the principal language for learning, deaf children must be provided separate, different services.

CONCLUSION

Legal processes set up inevitable linguistic tensions. Legislators are most comfortable choosing amorphous terms that can remain malleable over time (e.g., *effective, reasonable, qualified,* etc.). Executive agencies seek specificity when writing regulations so that they can be enforced with certainty. Judges seek specificity in their opinions so that they will apply to the particular controversy and parties before them.

In disability law, these three institutions have struggled among themselves to establish and define the key terms and the scope of the law. Congress adopted the broadest, most general statement of policy in the one sentence of Section 504. By 1990, Congress had learned from deaf and disabled advocates of the advisability of inserting highly specific provisions into the ADA. Executive agencies have also responded to public pressure. The disability community had a dramatic, confrontational, and volatile response to HEW's failure to adopt regulations for Section 504. In the ADA, Congress imposed a deadline for writing regulations, and the DOJ established a broad forum for public input into the content of the regulations. The Supreme Court has engaged in its traditional role of interpreting terminology, such as the definition of *a person with a disability*. The Court has limited the applicability of the ADA with its recent refinement of the term, eliminating protection for people who successfully use mitigating devices and medications.

The definitions of terms in disability law are affected by changing cultural understanding of the meaning of *disability*. The move in legal language from *handicap* to *disability* is meant to suggest that the persons protected by the law are not limited people. Deaf people have been especially vociferous in explaining that deafness is not a disability, that it has a cultural and linguistic core that is a source of pride and community cohesion. Nevertheless, to take advantage of the legal rights in the ADA and in Section 504, they must simultaneously accept the designation of *handicap/disability*.

As people with disabilities have moved in their own minds from recipients of social services to self-advocates, they have also appropriated civil rights rhetoric. The fit has not always been easy, since a person with a disability is by definition "different" from the dominant cultural or physical norm. The political arm of the disability advocacy community is eager to portray people with disabilities as strong and competent, fully able to take their place in the mainstream of the American economic and social system. They are eager to portray disability as a mainstream cultural norm. People without disabilities are sometimes labeled *temporarily able bodied* to create a cross-cultural community referent. This does not comport easily with the civil rights paradigm in which the groups entitled to protection from the dominant culture constitute a discrete and insular minority.

The most confusing aspect of placing disability rights in a civil rights framework is that some people with disabilities may need special or different services and accommodations to achieve equal opportunity in jobs, education, and social services. Strictly equal access does not provide equal opportunity for a person with a disability. Unlike race and gender discrimination, equal access for people with disabilities requires businesses and organizations to take extra, affirmative steps. They must spend money to hire interpreters, build elevators, and change procedures. Disability advocates face a challenge to define these "different" services so that they are properly seen as a foundation for equal opportunity rather than as an extra entitlement or preference. The Supreme Court's hostility to affirmative action means that the "affirmative steps" needed for equal opportunity are in some danger.

The most slippery term is that of *reasonable* accommodations in employment and *undue burden* on employers and businesses. For most judges, the reasonableness of an accommodation or a burden is measured solely by reference to the resources of the business or employer, not the need of the person with a disability. In cases involving deafness, judges find that they must engage in a multifaceted, fact-intensive inquiry, balancing the cost of the interpreter or other accommodation, the efficacy of the accommodation to achieve meaningful communication for a particular individual in a particular context, the importance and complexity of the communication scenario, and the benefits and burdens for the employer or business. There can be no certainty of outcome when a judge must balance so many competing factors.

There have been many successes in court as deaf plaintiffs have sought interpreters, captioning, and other communication services. However, other plaintiffs have failed to convince judges that they needed specific services. In the minds of deaf plaintiffs, the ADA is meant to guarantee equal communication to hearing people. It does not. In fact, the ADA has a much lower standard, that of effective communication. Similarly, IDEA does not guarantee deaf children an equal education; it provides only for an appropriate education. Confusion about these standards has caused frustration for deaf people trying to enforce the laws.

As more deaf people become politically involved and legally sophisticated, the laws continue to improve. Specific language has been adopted that is directly responsive to the efforts of deaf advocates. The best illustration of this is the new requirement that school officials consider special factors in the education of deaf children, including the child's ability to have direct communication with teachers. The Supreme Court is limiting the application of the ADA with an unusual sensitivity to intrusions into state political processes. However, whether decisions about legal standards are made at the federal or state level, Deaf community members must continue to step forward to ensure that their needs are addressed in the legal terminology chosen by the legal community.

NOTES

1. 309 U.S. 134, 138 (1940).

2. For many years, the *Pottsville* case has stood for the proposition that federal agencies, particularly the new agencies established during Franklin Roo-

sevelt's New Deal era, have significant authority to develop important policy in the course of writing regulations. Regulations cannot be written by federal executive agencies without express authority from statutes passed by Congress. However, *Pottsville* and subsequent cases acknowledged that executive agencies have the power and expertise to carry out congressional intent. As a result, Congress can establish broad policies and allow the executive agencies to determine the minutiae of regulatory language that will carry out this policy. See discussion at pages 98–102.

3. *Americans with Disabilities Act*, 38 U.S. Code (hereinafter referred to as U.S.C.), § 12101, et seq.; *The Rehabilitation Act of 1973*, Public Law 95-102, as amended. Section 504 of the Rehabilitation Act of 1973 is codified at 38 U.S.C. § 794; *Individuals with Disabilities Education Act (IDEA)*, 38 U.S.C. § 1401 et seq.

4. American law has extraterritorial effect in some limited situations. For example, employees of American companies who work abroad are still subject to the protections of the employment provisions of the ADA. Federal employees working abroad are protected by the employment provisions of Section 501 of the Rehabilitation Act of 1973, 38 U.S.C. § 791.

5. D. Sandburg, *The Legal Guide to Mother Goose*, (N.p.: Price Stern Sloan Publishers, 1979), 7–11.

6. Consent Decree, *DeVinney v. Maine Medical Center*, May 18, 1998, posted on the NAD Web site at http://www.nad.org/infocenter/infotogo/legal/devinney.html and on the DOJ ADA Web site at http://www.usdoj.gov/crt/ada/devin.htm. Similar language is now standard in settlement agreements negotiated by the DOJ. See, for example, *Settlement Agreement Under the ADA of 1990 Between the United States of American and St. Luke's Hospital and Health Network*, DOJ # 202-62-70, par. 49 (Sept. 10, 2001).

7. T. Goldstein and J. Lieberman, *A Lawyer's Guide to Writing Well*, (Berkeley: University of California Press, 1989), 19–20.

8. S. Burnham, *Drafting Contracts*, 2d ed. (Charlottesville, N.C.: Michie, 1993), 265.

9. NY CLS Ins § 3102 (2002). See also *New York Administrative Procedure Act*, NY CLS St Admin P Act § 201 (2002).

10. *Model Life and Health Insurance Policy Language Simplification Act*. National Association of Insurance Commissioners (1984).

11. Executive Order No. 12044, 43 *Code of Federal Regulations* (hereinafter referred to as C.F.R.) 12611.

12. *Securities Act Rule* 421(d). The new rule requires issuers to use "Plain English" in the organization, language, and design of the cover page, summary, and risk factor sections of their prospectuses. The language must, at a minimum, substantially comply with each of the following principles: the active voice; short sentences; definite, concrete, everyday words; tabular presentation or bulleted

lists for complex material; no legal jargon or highly technical business terms; and no multiple negatives.

13. D. Mellinkoff, *Legal Writing: Sense and Nonsense* (St. Paul, Minn.: West, 1982), 134.

14. J. Boyd, ed., *The Papers of Thomas Jefferson*, vol. 2 (Princeton: Princeton University Press, 1950), 230, as quoted in D. Mellinkoff, *The Language of the Law* (Boston: Little Brown, 1963), 252–53.

15. See, for example, 29 C.F.R. 33.6 (U.S. Department of Labor Section 504 regulation).

16. Other Latin phrases that are liberally used by American lawyers include *in personam, et al., in propria persona, ex parte* and *in forma pauperis*.

17. These forms tend to be based on the language that has been examined by the courts and ruled on in cases. Ironically, these are often the worst-drafted clauses and terms. If they were clearly written, there would be no question about what they mean, and no court would have to rule on them.

18. C. A. Hill, 2001. "Why Contracts Are Written in 'Legalese'" *Chicago-Kent Law Review* 77(1): 59–72.

19. T. Agostino, *Litigating ADA Claims: Forms, Pleading and Practical guidance.* (Horsham, Penn.: LRP Publications, 1996).

20. This concept is discussed in detail later in this paper. Legislators are given great leeway to pass laws and establish legislative classifications. However, when a law treats a suspect class differently from others, a court may strike the law down on constitutional grounds. Racial minorities, religious groups, and people who are of a foreign nationality are examples of groups that have been found to be suspect classes under the law. The Equal Protection Clause essentially requires state and federal governments to treat all similarly situated people alike. Therefore, a state law that singles out members of such a group and limits their rights is unconstitutional.

21. The term *suspect* was first used by the Supreme Court to describe a classification on the basis of race or nationality in *Korematsu v. United States*, 323 U.S. 214 (1944). That case was an unsuccessful challenge to the incarceration of Japanese-American citizens in concentration camps during World War II.

22. P. M. Tiersma, *Legal Language* (Chicago: University of Chicago Press, 1999), 106.

23. Ibid., 107–8.

24. *Rothschild v. Grottenthaler*, 907 F.2d 286 (2d Cir. 1990).

25. Mellinkoff, *The Language of the Law*, 290.

26. Mellinkoff, *Legal Drafting*, 15.

27. Mellinkoff, *The Language of the Law*, 331.

28. Ibid., 357–58.

29. Goldstein and Lieberman, *A Lawyer's Guide*, 21.

30. Ibid.

31. L. M. Solon, *The Language of Judges* (Chicago: University of Chicago Press, 1993), 12.

32. B. Cardozo, *The Nature of the Judicial Process* (New Haven: Yale University Press, 1921), 143, quoted in Solon, *Language of Judges*, 13.

33. *Communications Act of 1934*, Public Law 416, June 19, 1934, 73d Congress, codified at 47 U.S.C. § 151 et seq.

34. The resulting rule was codified at 47 C.F.R. 73.1250(h). This rule merely requires visual, as well as aural, transmission of emergency information, and captioning is one of the permissible methods of providing visual information. New captioning regulations are far more extensive, requiring closed captioning of virtually all new broadcasts by Jan. 1, 2006. See ibid, 79.1(b)(l)(iv).

35. National Association of the Deaf, *Legal Rights: The Guide for Deaf and Hard of Hearing People*, 5th ed. (Washington, D.C.: Gallaudet University Press, 2000), 187–203.

36. 47 C.F.R. 79.1(b)(l)(iv).

37. Closed Captioning Requirements for Digital Television Receivers; Closed Captioning and Video Description of Video Programming, Implementation of Section 305 of the Telecommunications Act of 1996, Video Programming Accessibility, ET Docket 99-254, MM Docket 95-176, Report and Order, FCC 00-259, 15 FCC Rcd 16788, 16790 (2000).

38. The definition of a "place of public accommodation" lists twelve specific types of commercial enterprises (place of lodging, establishment serving food or drink, sales or rental establishments, and so forth). Examples of each category are provided. If an entity does not operate within one of the specified categories, it is not subject to the ADA. However, within each category, the examples provided are illustrative and *not exhaustive*. For example, the category "sales and rental establishments" includes many facilities in addition to the examples provided, such as video stores, carpet showrooms, car dealerships, car rental establishments, pet stores, jewelry stores, realtors, and many more. *Department of Justice Title III Technical Assistance Manual*, III-1.2000 (Jan. 24, 1992); Department of Justice Analysis to Title III, *Federal Register*, 56, 35546 et seq.

39. 28 C.F.R. § 36.104.

40. See, for example, United States Department of Justice Policy Ruling, 9/9/96: ADA Accessibility Requirements Apply to Internet Web Pages, 10 National Disability Law Reporter 240.

41. Sen. Larry Craig, "The Americans with Disabilities Act: Prologue, Promise, Product and Performance," *Idaho Law Journal* 35 (1999): 205, 218.

42. Ibid., 205, 220.

43. For a comprehensive discussion of the legislative process in Congress, see "How Our Laws Are Made" by Charles W. Johnson, Parliamentarian of the U.S. House of Representatives, Jan. 31, 2000, at http://thomas.loc.gov/home/

lawsmade.toc.html. For the authoritative text of rules of the Congress, see *House Rules and Manual* (*Constitution, Jefferson's Manual, and Rules of the House of Representatives of the United States*), prepared by Charles W. Johnson, Parliamentarian of the House, House Document 105-358 (1999). New editions are published each Congress. *Senate Manual* (containing the rules, orders, laws, and resolutions affecting the business of the U.S. Senate; *Jefferson's Manual, Declaration of Independence, Articles of Confederation, Constitution of the United States*, etc.) prepared each session under the direction of Senate Committee on Rules and Administration.

44. There is a succinct case study of the passage of the Civil Rights Act of 1964 in William Eskridge and Philip Frickey, *Cases and Materials on Legislation—Statutes and the Creation of Public Policy* (St. Paul, Minn.: West, 1988).

45. After a bill is signed into law by the President, it is assigned a permanent set of numbers within the U.S. Code. A piece of legislative language may have been widely discussed and published with the numbering system used when it was still a bill (e.g., P.L. 94–142 or Section 504). However, lawyers and judges do not use these numbers unless they are referring to earlier versions of the law's language from its legislative history. Instead, they will call this language by its final number in the U.S. Code. Usually, a citation such as Section 504 means nothing to a practicing lawyer. That provision is correctly known as 29 U.S.C. 794 (Section 794 in the 29th title of the U.S. Code). In the case of disability laws, however, there was significant public education and discussion about the law at such an early stage that the bill numbers have stuck and are widely used, both by lay people and in courts.

46. Eskridge and Frickey, *Cases and Materials on Legislation*, 424.

47. 29 U.S.C. 794, as amended.

48. Craig, "The Americans with Disabilities Act," 205, 208 (1999), citing E. D. Berkowitz, "A Historical Preface to the Americans with Disabilities Act," *Journal of Policy History* 6 (1994): 96, 96–97. The history of the political machinations and the strategies used by disability advocates is ably presented in National Council on Disability, *Equality of Opportunity: The Making of the American with Disabilities Act.* (Washington, D.C.: National Council on Disability, 1997), 14–19.

49. *Cherry v. Mathews* 419 F.Supp. 922 (D.D.C. 1976).

50. 45 C.F.R. Part 84.

51. National Council on Disability, *Equality of Opportunity*, 14.

52. Ibid., 14.

53. R. K. Scotch, *From Goodwill to Civil Rights: Transforming Federal Disability Policy* (Philadelphia: Temple University Press, 1984), p. 156, quoted in National Council on Disability, *Equality of Opportunity*, 20.

54. *Erickson v. Board of Governors*, 207 F.3d 945, 2000 U.S. App. LEXIS 5074 (7th Cir Ill. 2000).

55. The need to gather supporting votes from the other members of the appellate panel does cause some judges to modify language choices to appeal to fellow judges. However, individual judges may also write separate concurring or dissenting opinions, or opinions that concur in part and dissent in part.

56. *Scott v. Sandford*, 60 U.S. (19 How.) 393, 404–06, 417–18, 419–20 (1857).

57. "That all persons born in the United States and not subject to any foreign power, excluding Indians not taxed, are hereby declared to be citizens of the United States; and such citizens, of every race and color, without regard to any previous condition of slavery or involuntary servitude . . . shall have the same right[s]. . . . " Ch. 31, 14 Stat. 27.

58. *Bolling v. Sharp*, 347 U.S. 497 (1954). The Fourteenth Amendment, which contains both an equal protection and a due process clause, applies to the states. By contrast, the Fifth Amendment, which applies to the federal government, contains only a due process clause. In *Bolling*, the Court ruled that "the concepts of equal protection and due process, both stemming from our American ideal of fairness, are not mutually exclusive. The 'equal protection of the laws' is a more explicit safeguard of prohibited unfairness than 'due process of law,' and, therefore, we do not imply that the two are always interchangeable phrases. But, as this Court has recognized, discrimination may be so unjustifiable as to be violative of due process." 347 U.S. 499.

59. Section 5 of the amendment empowers Congress to enforce this mandate by adopting legislation; but when Congress does not act, the courts have themselves devised standards for determining the validity of state legislation or other official action that is challenged as denying equal protection.

60. H. Peet, *Legal Rights and responsibilities of the Deaf and Dumb*, (Richmond, Va.: C. H. Wynne, 1857).

61. L. Myers, *The Law and the Deaf* (Washington, D.C.: U.S. Department of Health, Education and Welfare, 1967), 172.

62. Ibid., 20.

63. *Cleburne v. Cleburne Independent Living Center*, 473 U.S. 432, 440 (1985); *Schweiker v. Wilson*, 450 U.S. 221, 230 (1981); *United States Railroad Retirement Board v. Fritz*, 449 U.S. 166, 174 -175 (1980); *Vance v. Bradley*, 440 U.S. 93, 97 (1979); *New Orleans v. Dukes*, 427 U.S. 297, 303 (1976).

64. *Buck v. Bell*, 274 U.S. 200 (1927).

65. *Loving et ux v. Virginia*, 388 U.S. 1 (1967). The Lovings were arrested and charged with miscegenation. On January 6, 1959, the Lovings pleaded guilty to the charge and were sentenced to one year in jail; however, the trial judge suspended the sentence for a period of twenty-five years on the condition

that the Lovings leave the State and not return to Virginia together for twenty-five years. He stated in an opinion that:

Almighty God created the races white, black, yellow, malay and red, and he placed them on separate continents. And but for the interference with his arrangement there would be no cause for such marriages. The fact that he separated the races shows that he did not intend for the races to mix. 388 U.S. at 3.

66. 323 U.S. 214 (1944).
67. *Cleburne v. Cleburne Independent Living Center*, 473 U.S. 432, 439 (1985).
68. *Meyer v. Nebraska*, 262 U.S. 390 (1923).
69. Ibid., 402.
70. *Frontiero v. Richardson*, 411 U.S. 677, 681 (1973) (plurality opinion).
71. 411 U.S. 677, 686.
72. 163 U.S. 537 (1896).
73. Ibid., 543.
74. Ibid., 544.
75. Ibid., 559 (Harlan, dissenting).
76. 347 U.S. 483 (1954).
77. Ibid., 486–96.
78. Ibid., 494.
79. The prohibition against discrimination on the basis of sex appears only in the employment title of the act.
80. National Council on Disability, *Equality of Opportunity*, 10–11.
81. *City of Cleburne, Texas v. Cleburne Living Center*, 473 U.S. 432 (1985).
82. Ibid., 433.
83. Ibid., 432, 445.
84. Ibid., 440.
85. C. L. Ramsey *Deaf Children in Public Schools: Placement, Context, and Consequences*. (Washington, D.C.: Gallaudet University Press, 1997).
86. Ibid., 3.
87. Ibid., 2–3.
88. Ibid., 47–51.
89. Ibid., 50.
90. *Vocational Rehabilitation Act of June 2, 1920*, ch. 219, 41 Stat. 735 (codified as amended at 29 U.S.C. 731–41), (repealed in 1973 and reenacted in the *Rehabilitation Act of 1973*, Pub. L. No. 93–112, 87 Stat. 355).
91. National Council on Disability, *Equality of Opportunity*, 8–9.
92. *Congressional Record*, (1972): 118, 525–26.
93. See also S. Rep. No. 316, 96th Cong., 1st sess. 53 (1979) (attempting to amend Title VII of the Civil Rights Act by adding *disability* to the list of protected classes).

94. Craig, "The Americans with Disabilities Act," 205, 206.

95. *Rehabilitation Act of 1973*, P.L. 93-112, 93rd Cong., lst sess., (26 September, 1973), § 504 (codified as 29 U.S.C. 794). This provision was amended in 1978 to apply to federal executive agencies as well.

96. Craig, "The Americans with Disabilities Act," 205, 208 (1999), quoting Edward D. Berkowitz, "A Historical Preface to the Americans with Disabilities Act," *Journal of Policy History*, 6 (1994): 96, 96–97.

97. Scotch, *From Goodwill to Civil Rights*, 49–57, as discussed in National Council on Disability, *Equality of Opportunity*,14.

98. U.S. Constitution art. 1, § 8, cl. 1. "The Congress shall have the Power to lay and collect Taxes, Duties, Imposts and Excises, to pay Debts and provide for the common Defence and general Welfare of the United States . . . "

99. A related provision, Section 503, applies to federal contractors with contracts of over $2,500. 29 U.S.C. 793.

100. Interview, February 19, 1997, quoted in National Council on Disability, *Equality of Opportunity*, 26.

101. *Regents of the University of California v. Bakke*, 438 U.S. 265 (1978).

102. Sec. 2(a)(7), P. L. 101-336 (Findings and Purposes).

103. Sec. 2(b)(4), P. L. 101-336 (Findings and Purposes).

104. See, for example, *City of Boerne v. Flores*, 521 U.S. 507 (1997). Congress attempted to overturn a decision of the Supreme Court by enacting the Religious Freedom Restoration Act. The Supreme Court then ruled that the statute itself was unconstitutional and was not persuaded by the formal congressional findings about the constitutionality of the law. This case is not directly applicable to the ADA, but the Court has used *City of Boerne* to suggest that the ADA is also an inappropriate congressional act. See *Board of Trustees v. Garrett*, 531 U.S. 356 (2001).

105. A. Meyerson & S. Yee, "Facing the Challenges of the ADA: The First Ten Years and Beyond. The ADA and Models of Equality," *Ohio State Law Journal* 62(2001): 535, 536–37.

106. L. A. Montanaro, "The Americans with Disabilities Act: Will the Court Get the Hint? Congress' Attempt to Raise the Status of Persons with Disabilities in Equal Protection Cases," *Pace Law Review* 15(Winter, 1995): 621. This article discusses the case law before and after the *Cleburne* decision and the role the ADA may play in changing the Equal Protection analysis of laws affecting people with disabilities.

107. P.L. 99-506 (21 Oct. 1986), Title I, § 103(d)(2)(B) in part, Title X, § 1002(e)(4), 100 Stat. 1810, 1844.

108. P.L. 102-569 (29 Oct., 1992), Title I, Subtitle A, § 102(p)(32), Title V, § 506, 106 Stat. 4360, 4428.

109. 45 C.F.R. 84.3(j).

110. 42 U.S.C. 12112.

111. Craig, "The Americans with Disabilities Act," *Idaho Law Journal* 35 (1999): 205, 213.

112. M. Metzger, ed., *Bilingualism and Identity in Deaf Communities*, Sociolinguistics in Deaf Communities series, vol. 6 (Washington, D.C.: Gallaudet University Press, 2000).

113. *Emery v. Caravan of Dreams* (1995, ND Tex) 879 F.Supp. 640, 9 ADD 278, 4 AD Cas 409, aff'd without op. (1996, CA5 Tex) 85 F. 3d 622.

114. *Burns v. Coca-Cola Enters., Inc.*, 222 F. 3d 247 (6th Cir. 2000). Compare *Dupre v. Charter Behavioral Health Sys. of Lafayette, Inc.* 242 F. 3d 610 (5th Cir. 2001).

115. *Clemente v. Executive Airlines, Inc.*, 213 F. 3d 25, 10 (1st Cir. 2000).

116. See, for example, *Ellison v. Software Spectrum* 85 F. 3d 187, 16 ADD 942 (5th Cir 1996) or *EEOC v. R. J. Gallagher Co.* 181 F3d 645 (5th Cir. 1999).

117. 527 U.S. 471, 119 S.Ct. 2139 144 L.Ed.2d 450 (1999). See also *Murphy v. UPS*, 527 U.S. 516, 119 S.Ct. 2133, 144 L.Ed.2d 484 (1999). (A mechanic was not limited in major life activities when on his medication for hypertension.)

118. In *Sutton*, the Court struck down EEOC guidelines that required disability and limitation to be evaluated in an uncorrected or unmitigated state. 527 U.S. 483–84.

119. *Tangires v. Johns Hopkins Hosp.*, 79 F.Supp. 2d 587 (D.Md. 2000).

120. Civ. A No. 971649, 1999 WL 730498 (D. Ariz., Aug. 19, 1999).

121. 29 U.S.C. 791, 29 C.F.R. 1613.704.

122. Section 703(a)(1) of the Civil Rights Act of 1964, Title VII, 78 Stat. 255, 42 U.S.C. § 2000e-2(a)(1), and 2000e-2(j).

123. *Trans World Airlines, Inc. v. Hardison*, 432 U.S. 63, 84 (1977).

124. 42 U.S.C. § 12111(10). *See also* 29 C.F.R. § 1630.2(p). Factors relevant to a determination of undue burden include: (i) The nature and net cost of the accommodation needed under this part, taking into consideration the availability of tax credits and deductions, and/or outside funding; (ii) The overall financial resources of the facility or facilities involved in the provision of the reasonable accommodation, the number of persons employed at such facility, and the effect on expenses and resources; (iii) The overall financial resources of the covered entity, the overall size of the business of the covered entity with respect to the number of its employees, and the number, type and location of its facilities; (iv) The type of operation or operations of the covered entity, including the composition, structure and functions of the workforce of such entity, and the geographic separateness and administrative or fiscal relationship of the facility or facilities in question to the covered entity; and (v) The impact of the accommodation upon the operation of the facility, including the impact on

the ability of other employees to perform their duties and the impact on the facility's ability to conduct business.

125. H.R. Rep. No. 489(II), 65–66, 1990 U.S.C.C.A.N. 347–49 (emphasis added).

126. *Bryant v. Better Business Bureau*, 923 F. Supp. 720, 736–37 (D.Md. 1996).

127. Ibid., 740.

128. Ibid.

129. Public agencies are subject to Title II of the ADA. Private businesses and organizations are subject to Title III of the ADA. Title III requires covered entities to provide reasonable auxiliary aids and services necessary to allow a person with a disability to benefit from the said entity's goods and services. Thus, Title III requires covered entities to provide appropriate auxiliary aids and services for persons with hearing impairments, including interpreters, when such measures are necessary to ensure effective communication. 28 C.F.R. 36.303 (1999); Department of Justice, *The Americans with Disabilities Act: Title III Technical Assistance Manual* (Washington, D.C.: Author, 1993), 27 (hereinafter DOJ Title III). Title II requires a covered entity to "ensure that its communications with individuals with disabilities are as effective as communications with others." 42 U.S.C. 12182(b)(2)(A)(iii); Department of Justice, *The Americans with Disabilities Act: Title II Technical Assistance Manual* (Washington, D.C.: Author, 1993), 38. To ensure such effective communication, public entities must provide appropriate auxiliary aids and services, including qualified interpreters for individuals with hearing impairments.

130. No. 395-CV-02408 (AHN) (D. Conn. 1998) (consent decree), http://www.usdoj.gov/crt/ada/cthosp.htm.

131. 32 F. Supp. 2d 820; 1998 U.S. Dist. LEXIS 21650 (D.Md. 1998).

132. 908 F. 2d 740 (11th Cir. 1990). Other cases holding that colleges and universities must provide interpreters and other communication services are *Camenisch v. University of Texas*, 616 F. 2d 127 (5th Cir. 1980), vacated as moot, 451 U.S. 390 (1981); *Jones v. Illinois Department of Rehabilitation Services*, 504 F. Supp. 1244, fn. 56 (N.D. Ill. 1981), aff'd 689 F. 2d 724 (7th Cir. 1982); *Crawford v. University of North Carolina*, 440 F. Supp. 1047 (M.D.N.C. 1977); *Herbold v. Trustees of the California State Universities and Colleges*, C-78-1358-RHS (N.D. Cal. 1978), and *Barnes v. Converse College*, 436 F. Supp. 635 (D.S.C. 1977). See also Patrick *National Disability Law Reporter* 7:470.

133. *Gordon v. Texas et al.*, Civ. A. H-98–0394 (S.D. Texas, 1999). The settlement agreement is available at the NAD Web site at http://www.nad.org/infocenter/infotogo/legal/Gordonsettlement.html.

134. 166 F. Supp. 2d 316; 2001 U.S. Dist. LEXIS 16442 (W.D.Pa. 2001).

135. See also *Bravin v. Mount Sinai Medical Center*, 186 F.R.D. 293 (S.D.N.Y.

1999). A deaf father sought an interpreter during Lamaze classes offered by a hospital. The hospital objected, saying that the mother was their patient, not the father. The court ruled that the father was also receiving hospital services, needed to communicate, and was entitled to interpreter services.

136. 72 F. Supp. 2d 489; 1999 U.S. Dist. LEXIS 16773; 9 Am. Disabilities Cas. (BNA) 1761 (D.N.J., 1999).

137. 28 C.F.R. 35.104.

138. 296 Ill. App. 3d 127; 693 N.E.2d 1260; 1998 Ill. App. LEXIS 245; 230 Ill. Dec. 509 (1998).

139. 955 P.2d 528; 1998 Alas. App. LEXIS 14 (1998).

140. U.S. Department of Justice, *The Americans with Disabilities Act: Title III Technical Assistance Manual* (Supp. 1994), 6.

141. See, for example, *DeVinney v. Maine Med. Ctr.*, Civ. No. 97-276-P-C (D. Me. Nov. 6, 1998) (consent decree), http://www.usdoj.gov/crt/ada/devin.htm. Many examples of relevant case law are cited and discussed in Bonnie P. Tucker, "Access to Health Care for Individuals with Hearing Impairments," *Houston Law Review* 35 (2000): 1101, 1112–1115.

142. *City of Los Angeles v. Lyons*, 461 U.S. 95, 105 (1983).

143. 843 F. Supp. 1329 (N.D. Cal. 1994).

144. 1997 U.S. Dist. LEXIS 6616; 6 Am. Disabilities Cas. (BNA) 1345 (1997).

145. Tucker, "Access to Health Care," 1101, 1138, quoting from Bonnie Tucker, "Mental Health Services for Deaf Persons: Proposed Legislation," *Arizona State Law Journal* (1980): 673, 675–76.

146. Tucker, "Access to Health Care," 1101, 1139.

147. 864 F.Supp. 1201 (S.D. Fla. 1994).

148. Tucker, "Access to Health Care," 1101, 1142.

149. *Education for All Handicapped Children Act*, P. L. No. 94-142, 89 Stat. 773 (1975) (codified as amended at 20 U.S.C.A. secs. 1400-1487) (West Supp. 1997). In 1990, Congress changed the name of the act to the *Individuals with Disabilities Education Act*, Public Law 101-476, 104 Stat. 1141 (1990) (IDEA). See 20 U.S.C.A. § 1400(a) (1990).

150. D. M. Engel, "Law, Culture, and Children with Disabilities: Educational Rights and the Construction of Difference," *Duke Law Journal* (1991): 166.

151. *Brown v. Board of Education*, 347 U.S. 383, 393 (1954).

152. Ibid., 494.

153. Ibid., 496.

154. 20 U.S.C. 1400-1483 (1990), amended by 20 U.S.C.A. § 1400-1487 (West Supp. 1997).

155. R. W. Goldman, "A Free Appropriate Education in the Least Restrictive Environment: Promises Made, Promises Broken by the Individuals with Dis-

abilities Education Act," *Dayton Law Review* 20 (Fall, 1994): 243, 245 (footnotes omitted). See also Engel, "Law, Culture, and Children with Disabilities," 166, 176 ("In short, although the general purpose of the EHA was to provide children with disabilities an 'appropriate' education in the 'least restrictive environment,' both these goals remain vague in theory as well as in practice, with few guidelines to shape the substantive content of these newly articulated rights.").

156. See 20 U.S.C. 1400(b).

157. 20 U.S.C. 1401(a)(16), amended by 20 U.S.C.A. 1401(25). Specially designed instruction includes physical education and instruction in the classroom, the home, hospitals and institutions, and other settings.

158. Ibid 1401(a)(17), amended by 20 U.S.C.A. 1401(22). Related services include the early identification and assessment of disabling conditions in children, as well as:

> Transportation, and . . . developmental, corrective, and other supportive services (including speech-pathology and audiology services, psychological services, physical and occupational therapy, recreation, including therapeutic recreation, social work services, counseling services, including rehabilitation counseling, and medical services, except that such medical services shall be for diagnostic and evaluation purposes only).

159. 20 U.S.C. 1401(a)(20), amended by 20 U.S.C.A. 1401(11).

160. 20 U.S.C. 1412(2)(A) (1990), amended by 20 U.S.C.A. 1400-1487 (West Supp. 1997) (requiring states to establish a "goal of providing full educational opportunity to all [children with disabilities].")); S. Rep. No. 94-168, (1997), 9, (states must establish a goal to "guarantee that [children with disabilities] are provided equal educational opportunity.")

161. M. Weber, "The Transformation of the Education of the Handicapped Act: A Study in the Interpretation of Radical Statutes," *University of California–Davis Law Review* 24 (1990): 349, 366.

162. T. Eyer, "Greater Expectations: How the 1997 IDEA Amendments Raise the Basic Floor of Opportunity for Children With Disabilities," *Dickenson Law Review* 106 (1999): 613, 619.

163. *Board of Education v. Rowley*, 458 U.S. 176 (1982).

164. Ibid., 192. Justices White, Brennan, Marshall, and Blackmun disagreed. They believed that the IDEA was intended to provide equal educational opportunity. See ibid., 210–18.

165. Ibid., 192.

166. Ibid., 192 n.21.

167. "The educational opportunities provided by our public school systems undoubtedly differ from student to student, depending upon a myriad of factors that might affect a particular student's ability to assimilate information pre-

sented in the classroom. The requirement that States provide 'equal' educational opportunities would thus seem to present an entirely unworkable standard requiring impossible measurements and comparisons. Similarly, furnishing handicapped children with only such services as are available to nonhandicapped children would in all probability fall short of the statutory requirement of 'free appropriate public education'; to require, on the other hand, the furnishing of every special service necessary to maximize each handicapped child's potential is, we think, further than Congress intended to go. Thus to speak in terms of 'equal' services in one instance gives less than what is required by the Act and in another instance more. The theme of the Act is 'free appropriate public education,' a phrase which is too complex to be captured by the word 'equal' whether one is speaking of opportunities or services." Ibid., 199.

168. Ibid., n.11.

169. Ibid., 210.

170. 20 U.S.C.A. 1400(c)(1). See also H.R. Rep. No. 105-95, at 82 (1997) ("The purposes of the . . . Amendments of 1997 [include] promoting *improved educational results . . . through . . . educational experiences that prepare them for later educational challenges and employment . . . .*"); ibid., 84 ("This review and authorization of the IDEA is needed to move to the next step of providing special education and related services to children with disabilities: to *improve and increase* their educational achievement.").

171. *Individuals with Disabilities Education Act Amendments of 1997,* § 614(d)(3)(B)(iv).

172. Eyer, "Greater Expectations," 613, 634.

173. "Each of the amended [IEP] requirements clearly operates to encourage formulation of a more beneficial education program designed with high expectations for the child's success. For purposes of this discussion, there are three changes of particular significance. First, the new description of annual goals as 'measurable annual goals' confirms that such goals cannot be calculated to confer only an insignificant benefit. Second, the statement of educational services to be provided, or the means to the ends, must now be sufficient to allow the child to 'advance appropriately' toward the annual goals and 'progress' in the general curriculum. This new requirement for the statement of services calls for evaluation of the sufficiency of services. Third, the parental report cards are a new procedure intended to keep parents informed as to the sufficiency of their child's progress toward meeting the measurable annual goals. In a sense, the report card adds an element of accountability by alerting all parties when sufficient educational progress is not occurring. Each of these provisions is implicitly intended to ensure that each child's IEP is calculated to confer measurable progress rather than a trivial educational benefit." Ibid., 633–34. (footnotes omitted).

174. Ibid., 634–35.

175. Engel, "Law, Culture, and Children with Disabilities," 166, 167.

176. Ibid., 167.

177. Ibid., 188–89.

178. Ibid., 170, citing H.R. Conf. Rep. No. 94-664, 94th Cong., 1st sess. 43 (1975) and S. Rep. No. 168, 94th Cong., 1st Sess. 11, reprinted in 1975 *U.S. Code Congressional and Administrative News* 1425, 1435. (" . . . the frequent monitoring of a handicapped child's progress throughout the year is the most useful tool in designing an educational program for not only the child but those who are responsible for his management in school and at home. . . .).

179. Ibid., 176.

180. R. C. Smith, *A Case about Amy* (Philadelphia: Temple University Press, 1996).

181. Engel, "Law, Culture, and Children with Disabilities," 205.

Misunderstanding, Wrongful Convictions,

and Deaf People

George Castelle

Each of the previous papers in this book address a different issue, but a single theme recurs throughout: Miscommunication between those who are deaf and those who hear plagues the judicial process and can result in grave injustices.

In his paper, "The Language Problems of Minorities in the Legal Setting," Roger Shuy describes the difficulties of resolving legal disputes involving speakers of other languages and deaf people. He provides three troubling examples. First, a young Creole speaker from Hawaii was imprisoned for perjury on the basis of what appears to be a simple misunderstanding, which a linguist could have easily explained. In the second example, a Spanish immigrant was convicted for drug dealing on the basis of what appears to be a flawed translation, which a skilled linguist—or simply a better translator—could have easily corrected. The third example involves a deaf person's struggle with an unscrupulous salesman.

In the first two examples, the testimony of a linguist, if permitted in court, could have prevented disturbing instances of wrongful convictions and imprisonment based solely on the defendants' difficulties with communication in a traditional courtroom setting. The unwillingness of judges to permit the testimony of a linguist in both of these cases reflects an unfortunate misapplication of legal principles regarding expert testimony in general—a misunderstanding that occurs far too often in the American judicial system.

This paper is written from the perspective of an author who has extensive experience in practicing and teaching law, but who has no specialized training or knowledge of the legal problems of deaf people. In this paper, the author discusses his reactions, as well as the reactions of most courthouse personnel, as they encounter the problems of language and the law in Deaf communities.

Currently, two different legal tests are applied to testimony before it is considered admissible in American courts. These tests are applied to all expert testimony, regardless of whether it is from a linguist, a psychiatrist, a DNA analyst, a fingerprint technician, or anyone else who may express an expert opinion in court on the basis of education, training, or experience. Regardless of the test used, it should be clear that a linguist, or any other expert who can assist in clarifying misunderstandings, should routinely be permitted to testify in court cases involving speakers of other languages and deaf people.

The first test of expert testimony admissibility is the traditional *Frye* test, which is based on a 1923 ruling in the case of *Frye v. United States*. For expert testimony to be admissible under the *Frye* test, it must be based on a scientific theory or technique that is *generally accepted* by the relevant scientific community. In applying the traditional Frye test to the proposed testimony of a linguist, there can be little doubt that the theory and techniques applied by linguists are generally accepted and should be routinely admissible in legal proceedings at any time that their testimony would be helpful in resolving a legal issue.

In 1993, the *Frye* "general acceptance" test was abandoned by the U.S. Supreme Court and replaced in federal courts by a four-part "reliability assessment." Under the Court's ruling in *Daubert v. Merrell Dow Pharmaceuticals*, to be admissible in federal courts, the scientific theory or technique must be shown to be "reliable"—that is, scientifically sound. As guidance in making such a reliability assessment, the Court suggested four factors to assist in the inquiry:

1. Whether the theory or technique has been tested and found to be sound.
2. Whether it has been subjected to peer review and publication.
3. Whether, in respect to a particular technique, there is a high "known or potential rate of error" and whether there are "standards controlling the technique's operation"?
4. Whether the theory or technique enjoys "general acceptance" within the "relevant scientific community"? (As such, this fourth factor is a vestige of the old *Frye* standard.)

Upon the issuance of the *Daubert* decision in 1993, the four-part reliability assessment became immediately applicable to all federal court proceedings involving scientific testimony. In the years since 1993, the

Daubert standard has also been adopted by an increasing number of state courts.

Much like with the *Frye* analysis, in considering the testimony of a linguist in light of the *Daubert* criteria, it is difficult to comprehend a legal basis for judges to disallow the testimony of a linguist, especially in cases where misunderstandings in communication have such a clear bearing on the issue before the court. There is currently much litigation in American courts regarding the admissibility of expert testimony and the correct legal standards to be applied in making that determination. As clumsy as the legal system has sometimes been in correcting its own deficiencies, this recent wave of litigation and the heightened focus that it brings to these issues should eventually result in a reduced number of erroneous rulings. As expert testimony becomes more acceptable in clarifying and correcting problems of communication, fewer injustices that arise from miscommunication should occur in the future—both in and out of court.

Shuy's third example of communication difficulties in legal disputes involves a lawsuit arising from a deaf person's four-hour ordeal with an unscrupulous car salesman. In this case, the linguist was able to analyze the notes compiled during the four-hour transaction and reconstruct the probable sequence and meaning of what had occurred. In this example, in contrast to the first two, the judge permitted the testimony of the linguist. The difference in resulting verdicts is striking: The defendant received an award of six million dollars.

The first two examples were criminal cases, and the third was a civil case. Although it may not be appropriate to draw strong conclusions on the basis of this limited number of examples, it is worth noting that they seem to reflect a similar observation made by Sarah Geer in her paper, "When 'Equal' Means 'Unequal'—And Other Legal Conundrums for the Deaf Community," in which she explains the difficulties that deaf people encounter when they are arrested and denied an interpreter. As Geer explains, however, in similar circumstances in civil proceedings, deaf people have been much more successful.

Why are the courts so hostile to allowing interpreters and linguists to help deaf people during criminal cases, in contrast to the more favorable treatment they receive during civil cases? The answer may lie in the fundamental difference between how a person is received by the judicial system upon entry into criminal cases, as opposed to civil ones, a difference that may be exacerbated when the person is deaf.

In a criminal case, a person often enters the system without forewarning, after being abruptly arrested by a police officer. At the stationhouse or the courthouse, the police officer typically prepares the charging document, reciting only the officer's version of what occurred, while the arrested person is often hampered by handcuffs and restricted freedom of movement. Despite the theoretical presumption of innocence, in practice, an arrested person enters the system clothed in a presumption of guilt. A person who can communicate effectively can minimize the damage by quickly asserting available legal rights and safeguards. A person who cannot communicate effectively may appear no different than the career criminal who is caught red-handed; they both may appear to be asserting their right to remain silent, but for very different reasons. Unfortunately for the deaf defendant, the reason for remaining silent at the stationhouse can be easily misunderstood.

By contrast, a civil suit is ordinarily initiated in a far statelier manner. The timing and initial recitation of facts are selected by the person bringing the suit. More dignity is inherent in the process, and often juries sympathize with the aggrieved party. If communication difficulties occur, a defendant at least has time to address them before further misunderstandings happen.

The difficult problems facing deaf people in criminal cases are further explained by Rob Hoopes in his paper "Trampling *Miranda*: Interrogating Deaf People." Hoopes discusses how police interrogation can be a terrifying experience for the defendant, creating many opportunities for misunderstandings, misstatements, and manipulation. He explains that when the accused person is deaf, these problems are dramatically increased.

In the same paper, Hoopes discusses a study of the comprehensibility of legal communications when translated into American Sign Language (ASL). He focuses on the *Miranda* warnings and police interrogations, analyzing the comprehensibility of communications when the signed interpretations are provided by signers with beginner, intermediate, and advanced skills.

Hoopes finds that the signed interpretations of the beginning signers were uniformly incomprehensible. He finds that the signed interpretations of the intermediate signers are "incomprehensible" at worst, and "confusing" at best. This result will come as a surprise to most police officers, lawyers, and judges, who routinely assume that an interpreter with at least intermediate skills will be more than adequate for the purpose at hand.

Courthouse personnel will ordinarily have no training in dealing with communication problems involving deaf people. The legal and law enforcement communities will not know that translations into ASL do not involve literal, word-for-word translations from written or spoken English. Ordinarily, courthouse personnel will not know that ASL involves facial expressions and postures expressed simultaneously with manual signals.

It is little wonder that, as Hoopes explains, hearing individuals often mistake ASL facial expressions as expressions of emotion. The consequences can be much more severe in the legal system than in everyday life. In police training manuals, for example, officers are taught to study facial expressions and body postures during interrogation of suspects. In the standard police manual, Inbau et al.'s *Criminal Interrogation and Confessions*, extensive discussion is devoted to the evaluation of such nonverbal behavior. Even though it is often referred to as the "bible" of police interrogations, the manual does not contain a single reference to the interrogation of deaf people, let alone a discussion of the special communication issues involved.

The possible need for an interpreter is only mentioned once in the manual, and even then, the reference is to interpreters in general, and not to interpreters for deaf people. Furthermore, the reference to the interpreter only arises in the context of explaining where the interpreter should be seated in order to preserve the confrontational atmosphere in the interrogation room.

Additionally, police officers are trained to use trickery and deceit during interrogations. Although Inbau's manual cautions that force, the threat of force, and promises of leniency should be discouraged as interrogation tactics, the manual then states, "We do approve, however, of psychological tactics and techniques that may involve trickery and deceit."

The consequences of such police training and tactics can be severe, particularly when used against anyone who has difficulty communicating with officers. Misunderstandings are likely in the coercive atmosphere of a police interrogation room, even when difficulties in communication don't exist. When police insensitivity is combined with problems communicating with deaf people in such a setting, the risks of miscommunication are magnified many times over. As Shuy and Hoopes point out in both papers, the misunderstanding of as little as a single word can result in the wrongful conviction and imprisonment of an innocent defendant.

Hoopes points out a very basic fact, but one that is not widely understood in the legal community: ASL is a separate language, rather than a literal translation of spoken English into signed English. As basic as this point may be, most police officers, lawyers, and judges will not be aware of it. In their paper "Court Interpreting for Signing Jurors: Just Transmitting or Interpreting?" Mather and Mather expand on this significant point.

The authors discuss the need for accurate interpretation when a deaf person is called for jury duty. They explain the extensive confusion regarding exactly what constitutes "accuracy" in courtroom interpretation for jurors. Neither judges nor lawyers will understand that ASL is a separate language of its own, combining manual signals, facial expressions, and body postures, and that, consequently, translating into ASL does not—and cannot—involve literal word-for-word translation. As Mather and Mather point out, however, the need to achieve "legal equivalence," rather than verbatim translation, will nonetheless require the translator to accomplish the enormously complex task of translating in a manner that also conveys the speaker's nuances and level of formality, including the speaker's style, tone, intent, hesitation, emotion, and demeanor.

Many jury trials involve judging the credibility of those who testify. The result of a major criminal or civil trial can turn on the jury's assessment of the truthfulness of a single statement expressed by one key witness. An error in interpretation—or an incorrectly expressed nuance—can result in a misunderstanding that could be fatal to an entire case. In light of this danger, it is discouraging to note that, despite the complexity of accurate interpreting, the task in many courtrooms may be assigned to interpreters with skill levels that Hoopes's study would find to be nearly incomprehensible.

Unfortunately, the more we study the problem, the worse it appears to be. In the previous paper, Geer points out that the legal meanings of some words can be very different from their meanings in ordinary English. The complexity of legal language sometimes introduces, in effect, a third language into the courtroom proceedings: (1) spoken English, (2) ASL, and (3) "legalese." The challenge of accurately translating spoken English into ASL is difficult enough. The challenge of translating convoluted and archaic legal language into ASL seems almost insurmountable.

At one time, there was a certain logic to what now appears to be archaic and sometimes incomprehensible legalese. Even simple redundancies such as the term *will and testament* served an important purpose centuries ago, when Britain was inhabited by various groups (Angles, Saxons, Normans) who spoke a variety of languages. To be understood by all speakers, it made sense in that era to express legal terms using both a word with a Germanic root (understandable by Anglo-Saxons) followed by a synonym with a Latin root (understandable by Normans).

That era, of course, has long since passed. Unfortunately, the use of archaic legalisms did not disappear when the need for them disappeared. Regardless, it should be understood that the convoluted and archaic legal language that Geer describes is not "good" legal language, anymore than it is good English.

The purpose of a legal document is to avoid litigation, not to cause it. Consequently, to serve its intended purpose, a carefully drafted legal document should be written in clear and understandable language. Unfortunately, many law school graduates promptly succumb to the temptation to draw legal language from established legal forms in old and sometimes archaic formbooks. Other new lawyers simply model their legal work on the examples set by the senior lawyers in the firm, who themselves borrow language from archaic formbooks or from even more senior lawyers a generation before.

Old legal habits are difficult to break. Even lawyers who understand the importance of clear speech will still enter the courtroom and fall into the familiar pattern of legal mumbling that is comprehensible only to the judge and opposing counsel.

For courthouse personnel, one of the most important lessons to be gleaned from this book is that the risk of injustice is substantially more severe when one of the persons participating in the proceeding is deaf. The injustices that Shuy and Hoopes describe could be minimized or avoided altogether in the future. Similarly, the equality of opportunity that Mather and Mather and Geer discuss can also be achieved, or at least approximated. To accomplish these goals, the legal system must respond to the points made by the authors and (1) acquire a larger and more skilled pool of translators, (2) use clear and unambiguous legal language in all proceedings, and (3) develop an increased awareness of the special problems related to communicating with deaf people during courtroom proceedings.

REFERENCES

1. *Frye v. United States*, 54 App.D.C. 46, 293 F. 1013 (1923).
2. *Daubert v. Merrell Dow Pharmaceuticals*, 509 U.S. 579 (1993).
3. *Miranda v. Arizona*, 384 U.S. 436 (1966).
4. F. E. Inbau, J. E. Reid, J. P. Buckley, and B. C. Jayne. 2001. *Criminal interrogation and confessions*, 4th ed. Gaithersburg, Md.: Aspen Publishers.
5. S. D. Westervelt and J. A. Humphrey, eds. 2001. *Wrongly convicted: Perspectives on failed justice*. New Brunswick, N.J.: Rutgers University Press.

Contributors

George Castelle is the Chief Public Defender in Charleston, West Virginia, and is an adjunct lecturer at the West Virginia University College of Law in Morgantown. In 1997, he won the National Legal Aid and Defender Association's Reginald Heber Smith award for his work in exposing fraud in the West Virginia State Police Crime Lab and freeing prisoners who had been wrongfully convicted by erroneous forensic science. In addition to an active practice representing indigent defendants, he frequently speaks at continuing legal education seminars on numerous topics, including forensic science, eyewitness testimony, legal ethics, trial techniques, appellate advocacy, wrongful convictions, psychology and the law, juvenile delinquency, habeas corpus, evidence, and criminal procedure.

Sarah S. Geer is an attorney in northern Virginia. For over twenty years, she was a part of the National Association of the Deaf Law Center and the National Center for Law and Deafness at Gallaudet University. In addition to advising the National Association of the Deaf on legal policy issues, she represented deaf and hard of hearing individuals in cases under the ADA, Section 504 of the Rehabilitation Act, and federal education law. She is a co-author of *Legal Rights: The Guide for Deaf and Hard of Hearing People* (Washington, D.C.: Gallaudet University Press, 2002) and other articles on disability law issues. She is a graduate of Oberlin College and the University of North Carolina School of Law.

Rob Hoopes holds a J.D. from the University of Cincinnati. He subsequently earned a master's degree in linguistics from Gallaudet University and is currently a doctoral fellow at Georgetown University. He also holds a Certificate of Interpretation from the Registry of Interpreters for the Deaf.

Robert Mather is a senior trial attorney in the Disability Rights Section of the Civil Rights Division of the Department of Justice. This section is responsible for the enforcement of the Americans with Disabilities Act (ADA), which prohibits discrimination on the basis of disability. He received a J.D.

from DePaul University Law School. He was born deaf and uses sign language to communicate.

Susan Mather is a professor at Gallaudet University, Graduate School and Professional Studies, Department of Linguistics. She received a master's degree in linguistics at Gallaudet University and a Ph.D. in sociolinguistics from Georgetown.

Roger W. Shuy is Distinguished Research Professor of Linguistics, Emeritus, at Georgetown University, where he created the sociolinguistics program and taught for thirty years. His specializations are sociolinguistics and forensic linguistics. His most recent books include *Linguistic Battles in Trademark Disputes; The Language of Confession, Interrogation and Deception; Bureaucratic Language in Government and Business;* and *Language Crimes.* He now resides in the beautiful mountain area of Missoula, Montana.

Index

Hawaiian Creole speaker, legal problems of, 2–5, 17, 168
Health services and effective communication, 135, 139–40
Hearing aids, 127–28
Hewitt, W.E., 69
Holmes, Oliver Wendell, 108

IDEA. *See* Individuals with Disabilities in Education Act
Illinois v. Long (1998), 137–39
Inbau, F. E., 172
Individualized education programs (IEPs), 145, 148, 149–52
Individuals with Disabilities in Education Act (IDEA), 19, 83, 111, 143–52
  amendments of 1997, 147–48
  direct communication under, 148
  individualized education programs (IEPs), 145, 148, 149–52
  Rowley case construing, 145–47
Injunctive relief under ADA Title III, 140
Insurance law and plain English requirements, 88
Internet, 96–97
Interpreters
  accuracy as standard for, 72, 74, 137, 173
  certified, 64–65, 135
  confidentiality and, 141
  court interpreting, 69–72
  effective communication. *See* Effective communication
  failing to keep up with English speaker, 34
  inadequacy of, 34, 45, 134–35, 141–43
  interview interpreting, 69, 70
  for jurors, 19, 60–81. *See also* Jurors, interpreting for
  "legal equivalence" as goal of, 70, 78
  mental health setting, 141–43

for *Miranda* warnings and interrogation of Deaf suspect. *See* Interrogation of Deaf suspects; *Miranda* warnings
  nonmanual signals and, 33–34
  for parties at trial, 18
  proceedings interpreting, 69
  qualified, defined, 64–65
  research studies of, 34–45
  at school meetings for Deaf parents, 92–93, 150
  style of speech to be conveyed by, 71
  summary mode of translation, 70
  transliterating, 68
  witness interpreting, 69–70
Interrogation of Deaf suspects, 18–19, 21–59, 170–73. *See also* *Miranda* warnings
  arrests and, 24–26
  case study during criminal prosecution, 23, 45–49
    ethnographic description and findings, 46–49
    method, 45–46
  false statements, 21
  Fifth and Sixth Amendment constraints, 26–28
  interpreters for, 22, 28
    police officers with limited ASL skills, 23
  language issues, 28–34
  police power, 21, 23–24
  research study of native judgments of comprehensibility, 42–45
    findings, 44–45
    method, 42–44
  research study of nonmanual signals, 22–23, 34–42
    audiotape transcript, 53–54
    findings and discussion, 38–42
    frequency of signals by subject, 40–41, 55–59
    method, 22–23, 35–38
Interview interpreting, 69, 70

Jargon. *See* Legal language
Jefferson, Thomas, 89
Johnson v. Zerbst (1938), 27
Judicial Conference of the Administrative Office of the United States Courts, 66
Judicial process and interpretation of law, 102–4
Judicial system. *See* Justice system
Jurors, interpreting for, 19, 60–81, 173
 access to courts, 61–66
  federal law, 61–65
  state law, 65–66
 accuracy as standard for, 72, 74, 173
 auxiliary aids and services, 63–65
 court interpretation, 69–72
  standards for, 70–72
  types and functions of, 69–70
 English literacy requirement for jurors, 66–67, 77
 examples of jury service, 72–76
 legal background, 61–67
 "legal equivalence" as goal of, 70, 78
 New York Superior Court case on use of interpreters (*People v. Guzman* (1984)), 72–75, 76–78
 oath for interpreter, 75, 79
 Pennsylvania experience, 75–76
 recommendations, 78–79
 role of interpreter, 77
 sign language, 67–69
  ASL and contact signing, 67–68
  interpreting, 68–69
 Signed English, preference for, 72, 75, 76, 77
Justice, Department of
 settlement agreements with, 65
 Title II Technical Assistance Manual Covering State and Local Government Programs and Services, 63–64

Justice system. *See also* Criminal justice system
 Deaf person's understanding of, 45
 interpretation of law as role of, 102–4
 purpose and procedures of, 23–24

Korematsu v. United States (1944), 109

Language, legal. *See* Legal language
Lee, Randy, 75–76
Legal language, 82–167, 173–75
 archaic terminology and ritualistic language, 88–90
 attorneys' fondness for, 87
 characteristics of, 84–98
 child custody cases, 94–95
 development of, 98–104
  executive process, 99–102
  judicial process, 102–4
  legislative process, 98–99
 dictum, 92–93
 effective communication. *See* Effective communication
 equality, meaning of, 104–14
 formbooks and, 90–91
 notice requirements, 85–87
 obscurity, 85–87
 plain English requirements, 86–88
 precision of, 93–94
 problems presented by, 1–2, 16–20, 82–84, 173–75
 redundancy, 93
 search and seizure, 95
 stare decisis, 90, 103
 telecommunications law, 95–96
 terms of art, 90–93
 vagueness of, 94–98
 wills and, 93–94
 written codes of, 88–89
Legal system. *See* Justice system
Legislative process and enactment of statutes, 98–99
Liddell, S., 30

Nonmanual signals (*continued*):
  questions, 31, 40, 41
  research findings and discussion,
    38–42
  research method, 37–38
  topicalization, 32–33, 41
Notice requirements, 85–87

Oath for interpreter, 75, 79
Obscurity of legal language, 85–87

Parents
  IEP process and, 149–52
  interpreters for Deaf parents at
    school meetings, 92–93, 150
Pennsylvania experience with signing
    jurors, 67
People v. See name of opposing party
Pidgin Signed English, 68, 78
Pilots and vision impairment cases un-
    der ADA, 127
Places of public accommodation, 96–
    97, 140
Plain English requirements, 86–88
Plessy v. Ferguson (1896), 112–13
Police interrogation of Deaf suspects,
    18–19, 21–59. *See also* Interro-
    gation of Deaf suspects
Police power
  arrest, 21
  human rights and, 23–24
  interrogation, 21. *See also* Interro-
    gation of Deaf suspects
Precedent, use of, 90, 103
Probable cause, 24
Proceedings interpreting, 69
*Proctor v. Prince Georges Hospital
    Center* (1998), 133
Public accommodation. *See* Ameri-
    cans with Disabilities Act of
    1990 (ADA)
Public defenders, 26–27

Questions and syntactic nonmanual
    signals, 31, 40, 41, 55–59

Racial discrimination and Equal Pro-
    tection, 105–7
  suspect classification, 108–9,
    111–14
Ramsey, Claire, 117–18
Reasonable accommodation, 128–32,
    154
  Deafness and, 130–32
  legal language and, 97
"Reasonable man standard," 94
Redundancy of legal language, 93
*Regents of the Univ. of California v.
    Bakke* (1978), 121–22
Registry of Interpreters for the Deaf
    (RID), 135
Regulation promulgation, 99–102
Rehabilitation Act of 1973, Section
    504, 19, 83, 120–21
  applicability of, 121
  change from "handicapped" to
    "persons with disabilities," 89,
    123–24
  compared to Civil Rights Act, 121
  effective communication. *See* Effec-
    tive communication
  notice requirements, 85–87
  reasonable accommodation, 128–
    32. *See also* Reasonable accom-
    modation
  regulations promulgated under,
    100–102, 120
  sign language interpreter for Deaf
    parents at school meetings,
    92–93, 150
Rehabilitation services, 119
Religious discrimination
  hardship on employer and, 129
  scholarships and, 106
Remedies
  ADA Title III, public accommoda-
    tion, 140
  disability cases under Equal Protec-
    tion, 116–18
Rhode Island law
  interpreters for Deaf jurors, 66